"The greatest pleasure of a dog is that you may make a fool of yourself with him, and not only will he not scold you, but he will make a fool of himself, too."

—SAMUEL BUTLER, *Author*

"I think dogs are the most amazing creatures; they give unconditional love. For me they are the role model for being alive."

—GILDA RADNER, *Comedian*

"Folks will know how large your soul is, by the way you treat a dog."

—CHARLES F. DORAN, *Author, Academic and Political Expert*

"Petting, scratching, and cuddling a dog could be as soothing to the mind and heart as deep meditation and almost as good for the soul as prayer."

—DEAN KOONTZ, *Author*

"Dogs do speak, but only to those who know how to listen."

—ORHAN PAMUK, *Author*

Praise for the *What the Pet Food Industry Is Not Telling You*

"Krol debuts with an impassioned treatise on using holistic nutrition to ensure the longevity of our pets." —Book Life Reviews

"A fascinating read which feels well-researched and honest. I'd recommend it to anybody who has an open mind to pet ownership.'" —The Wishing Shelf International REVIEW

"For pet owners who are interested in administering such a raw food diet, Krol provides justification and sufficient information for anyone to easily execute the plan." —Kirkus Reviews

"This book aims to share that knowledge with other dog owners, too. In the process, it often references Krol's dog's success story, but also the pain that she saw him go through before his transition to the book's plan." —Clarion Reviews

"Passionate about the subject, Krol manages to be conversational and convincing at the same time and delivers copious information, including interesting facts like, "your dog has stomach acid that is over ten times more potent than what us humans have." —Blue Ink Review

"The author Stephanie Krol is brilliant and has done so much research because of her love for animals and her love for her own dog who was given only 3-4 months to live." —Amazon Reviewer MM

"I learned a lot to save my 11 years old black lab from reading this awesome book." —Amazon Reviewer Marissa

"This is a very easy to read and conversational approach that all pet owners need to read relative to the traditional pet food industry and the traditional veterinary industry." —Amazon Reviewer David

Awards for the *What the Pet Food Industry Is Not Telling You*

Global Book Award Winner, 2024, Silver Award for Education and Reference

2023 FIREBIRD BOOK AWARD, Winner of the two categories: Reference, and Diet & Nutrition — Animal/Pet and 2nd place Winner of Animal/Pet Semi-finalist

BookLife Prize 2023

Midwest Book Awards (Silver-Finalist) 2023, Nonfiction Business

WINNER 2022 INDEPENDENT PRESS AWARD (IPA), Distinguished Favorite — Animals–Pets

WINNER 2022 INDEPENDENT BOOK PUBLISHERS ASSOCIATION (IBPA), Benjamin Franklin Award — Animal & Pet Silver

2021 & 2022 NATIONAL & INTERNATIONAL Best Seller Amazon

WINNER 2022 LIVING NOW BOOK AWARDS (IPPY), Gold Medal Winner — Animal/Pets

WINNER 2022 NYC BIG BOOK AWARD (GABBY Book Awards), Animal — Pets Nonfiction & NYC 2022 BIG BOOK AWARD, Distinguished Favorite for Book Cover in Nonfiction category

FINALIST 2022 THE IAN BOOK OF THE YEAR AWARDS, The Independent Author Network

NFAA GOLD WINNER 2022 NONFICTION AUTHORS ASSOCIATION (NFAA), Gold Medal Winner- Animals/Pets

indieBRAG, B.R.A.G. Medallion Honoree 2022 WINNER

WINNER 2022 NONFICTION AUTHORS ASSOCIATION (NFAA), Gold Medal Winner — Animals/Pets

WHAT THE PET FOOD INDUSTRY IS NOT TELLING YOU

Developing GOOD PRACTICES for a HEALTHIER DOG

DR. STEPHANIE KROL
CHWC, AFMC, CRDFNS, and CAPPB

Professional Status and Member of the International Association of Canine Professionals and Certified with the Commission for the Association of Drugless Practitioners

What The Pet Food Industry Is Not Telling You: Developing Good Practices for A Healthier Dog
Published by: Riley Publishing
Wheaton, IL

Copyright ©2021 by Dr. Stephanie Krol. All rights reserved.

No part of this book may be reproduced in any form or by any mechanical means, including information storage and retrieval systems without permission in writing from the publisher/author, except by a reviewer who may quote passages in a review.

All images, logos, quotes, and trademarks included in this book are subject to use according to trademark and copyright laws of the United States of America.

Publisher's Cataloging-in-Publication data

Names: Krol, Stephanie, author.
Title: What the pet food industry is not telling you : developing good practices for a healthier dog / Dr. Stephanie Krol.
Description: Updated version. | Wheaton, IL: Riley Publishing, 2023.
Identifiers: ISBN: 978-1-7373201-9-7 paperback, 978-1-7373201-3-5 hardcover
Subjects: LCSH Dogs--Food. | Dogs--Nutrition. | Dogs--Food--Recipes. | Pet food industry. | BISAC PETS / Food and Nutrition
Classification: LCC SF427.4 .K76 2023 | DDC 636.7/085--dc23

Cover and Interior Design by Victoria Wolf, wolfdesignandmarketing.com
Editing by Jennifer Jas, wordswithjas.com

QUANTITY PURCHASES: Schools, companies, professional groups, clubs, and other organizations may qualify for special terms when ordering quantities of this title. For information, email: questions@catalystgroupsolutions.com.

All rights reserved by: Dr. Stephanie Krol and Riley Publishing.
Printed in the United States of America.

This book is dedicated to all the loving dog parents like you who want to do their absolute best for the dogs they madly love and consider part of their family. I hope this book guides you in making the very best decisions for your dog and stops the unnecessary toxicity and pain of dogs and cats around the world!

DISCLAIMER

DR. STEPHANIE KROL encourages each reader to do their own research and work with qualified professionals when making any decision related to their health. Dr. Krol is an Educator with a Doctorate in Education (Ed.D.) and is a Certified Health and Wellness and Functional Medicine Coach, as well as a Licensed Real Estate Broker. Dr. Krol is not a Medical Doctor (M.D.). The contents of this book are provided solely for informational and educational purposes. No information in this book is intended or designed to cure, diagnose, manage, or prevent any disease/s. Likewise, this book is not a substitute for professional medical advice. The author of this book does not guarantee the accuracy or completeness of the information presented, and disclaims any liability for any loss, damage, or injury that may result from its use. The statements in this book have not been evaluated by the FDA, and any links to third-party websites are provided for reference only, and do not represent an endorsement of their content or products. Neither the author or this book have the intention or purpose of giving medical advice. Readers are advised to consult with a licensed healthcare professional for any health-related concerns. The views and opinions expressed in this book are not intended to replace conventional medical advice and/or services. If your pet has a severe medical condition, please seek the advice of a licensed healthcare practitioner that you know and trust.

CONTENTS

DISCLAIMER — vii
PREFACE — xi
THIS BOOK IS FOR YOU BECAUSE … — xiii
INTRODUCTION — xvii
FROM THE AUTHOR — xxi

CHAPTER 1
A Better Path to Pet Health — 1

CHAPTER 2
What the Pet Industry Doesn't Want You to Know — 27

CHAPTER 3
Breaking Down Disease — 39

CHAPTER 4
Why are Certain Veterinarians Adverse to a Species Appropriate Diet? — 51

CHAPTER 5
Transitioning Your Dog's One-Chambered Stomach — 79

CHAPTER 6
Learning About a Species Appropriate Diet and How It Works — 87

CHAPTER 7
What Types of Foods Do Most People Feed on a Species Appropriate Diet? — 117

CHAPTER 8
Species Appropriate Diet Examples and Guidelines   139

CHAPTER 9
Dog Chew Choices and Making Your Own Training Treats   169

CHAPTER 10
How Do I Determine the Proper Weight for My Dog?   179

CHAPTER 11
Variety and Emotional Feeding   189

CHAPTER 12
Puppies and a Species Appropriate Diet   199

CHAPTER 13
Cats and a Species Appropriate Diet   207

CHAPTER 14
Resources and More Information   215

AFTERWORD
The Rest of the Story…   219

REFERENCES   223
AFFILIATE DISCLAIMER   247
ABOUT THE AUTHOR   249

PREFACE

THIS BOOK WAS WRITTEN OUT OF THE MAD LOVE I have for my dog, my previous dogs, and for dogs around the world. The pain and trauma I felt in the traditional medical system while trying to make the right choice for my dog when I was faced with a serious situation relative to my dog's health pushed me to write this book. I wrote it for others going through those same situations, who also are unsure where to turn and which method of treatment is best. I want to pay it forward to those who have helped me heal my dog. Each chapter is a thank you to those who helped me make the best decisions for my dog.

In this book, my goal is to share the knowledge I gained in healing my dog. My hope is that it will spare all dogs from pain all over the world. Hopefully, it will help you glean the information you need to help your dog live the longest, happiest life possible. Given my love for dogs and horses and knowing how much my dogs have given to me throughout my life, I feel great joy and happiness just knowing I can make a positive difference in another dog's life.

This book is also dedicated to my mom. She always pushed me to be my best and do my best. She literally expected me to know everything about everything! It has made me the strong, relentless person

I am, especially when facing something important to me, because I do not stop until I have exhausted all options or looked at all options to do my best. Thank you to my late father and my mom for making me work for everything I got and to always push me to keep moving forward and bettering myself educationally, as well as personally. There is such great value and success in hard work well done!

THIS BOOK IS FOR YOU BECAUSE ...

AS A DOG OWNER, YOU WILL LEARN about a unique nutrition plan that is designed to optimize your dog's health and lifespan. This comprehensive plan includes food lists, do's and don'ts, weekly schedules, and more.

This well-researched book covers knowledge gained from health science, holistic methodology, functional medicine, nutritional standards, and health coaching relative to dogs and humans. And guess what? It is all presented in a user-friendly and easy-to-understand style.

The dream is to empower dog owners with the exact knowledge and strategies they need so their pets can live their lives as happy and healthy as possible. This book is for cat owners too. While I primarily address dogs, see Chapter 13 for specific information about adapting this information for cats.

Book Summary for Pet Owners

This book is for you if you want your dog to live a genuinely healthy life.

- You're no longer willing to put toxins on or in your dog.
- You want a nutrition plan that can prevent disease, reduce disease, and put diseases into remission.
- You want a science-based and common-sense approach to pet health, wellness, and nutrition.
- You want to discover the truth about the pet feed industry and veterinarian industry.
- You are willing to raise your awareness and gain insights about how to increase your dog's health, wellness, and vitality.

Dog Health and Wellness

- Learn how to restore your pet's health.
- Learn how to build their immune systems, so they don't get sick in the first place.
- Learn how to reverse disease and restore your dog's health through diet.
- Learn how to keep a puppy or newly rescued pet healthy or reverse disease.

My dream is for veterinarians, clinic owners, and veterinary professors at colleges and universities to gain the exact knowledge and strategies they need so their clients' dogs can live their lives as happy and healthy as possible.

Book Summary for Universities, Vets, and Clinic Owners

Are you a veterinarian or studying to become one? Do you own an animal clinic? This book is for you if:

- You want to show your clients how their dogs can live a genuinely healthy life.
- You want to be able to teach your clients how to stop putting toxins on or in their dogs.
- You want to learn a science-based nutrition plan that can prevent disease, reduce disease, and put diseases into remission.
- You want a common-sense approach to pet health, wellness, and nutrition that you can simply and easily share with dog owners.
- You want to be fully informed and know the full truth about the pet feed industry and traditional veterinarian industry.
- You are willing to raise your awareness and gain insights about how to increase the health, wellness, and vitality of dogs and cats.

Dog Health and Wellness

- An anatomy of dog digestive and nutritional health
- A look at what the research says about nutrition and commercialized dog feed
- New vaccination schedule suggestions
- Vaccination schedules and toxicity
- A guide for dog owners on commercialized pet feeds
- Anatomy of a dog's gut and nutritional needs
- How to help pet owners heal their pets
- A guide for general health and wellness in dogs
- Parents who want the best for their dogs

INTRODUCTION

THE VETERINARY AND COMMERCIAL PET FOOD INDUSTRY has come a long way with health and wellness overall over the decades. As the years go on, industries progress. They learn and grow from our history and previous knowledge gained. Growing and becoming our best as individuals/professionals and utilizing technology and pharmaceuticals to their greatest extents are in essence what humans are taught to do from school-age on and after they enter their professions. In a smaller number of cases, those skills are necessary to preserve life when tragedy and extreme situations strike.

So many new technologies and preventative testing methods have emerged recently. These can help give dogs greater and healthier lives. Even many pet feeds and veterinary practices have transitioned into less chemically oriented food choices for pets. This shift has paralleled our human food choices and medical testing in the United States, which have equally moved toward preventative testing. More holistic and organic food choices for humans and pets are now abundantly available. These can serve to extend our lives and, in many cases, place diseases into remission.

The veterinary and commercialized pet feed industry is noticing the demand from pet owners and consumers to take the best care of our pets. Specifically, they are beginning to understand our precious dogs more deeply. These beautiful animals we love and cherish are most definitely the center of our families. In most cases, they make our house a home. This book endeavors to raise the level of awareness for dog health and wellness. It merges information from the two industries mentioned earlier into a pragmatic way for pet owners, professionals, and industries to speak the same language about dog health, wellness, nutrition, disease prevention, and remission.

It's liberating to learn or even consider that a difference between pet food and pet feed exists. Processing food out of its raw state of any kind changes it into feed, instead of real food. Real food is nutritionally intact with all the enzymes, molecules and nutrient levels present. When food is altered by cooking, pressurizing, and other methods, bodies (human or animal) innately are not processed correctly. This creates waste that the body has to deal with. If not correctly eliminated or resolved, this can lead to disease states I talk about in this book.

This book holds and advocates a common-sense approach to pet health, wellness, and nutrition. It can be added to all veterinary program curriculum, studied by holistic veterinarians in their practice, and read by traditional veterinarians who want to hear the latest research to implement into their practice. This newfound knowledge relative to the pet feed industry can create a bridge from the traditional veterinary industry to provide a platform for updated vaccination protocols, health and wellness applications, and the research around them. It can also assist with nutritional suggestions for clients and pet owners who are looking for a wellness approach versus a traditional drug-based approach to pet health and wellness. It can also expand the options vets can offer clients to help reverse and possibly put into remission disease states.

Lastly, this book can also create a greater understanding of pet wellness and health and nutrition for the pet feed industry. It gives a greater understanding of dog anatomy and nutritional needs and includes new ways to create proper food choices and how to mix them for pets around the world. This method can prevent disease and restore health that has already been burdened by toxicity and incorrect feeding choices.

The goal is to create a platform for conversation for pet owners, the veterinary industry, and the commercialized pet feed industry. The plan is to encourage healthy steps forward with knowledge that can be implemented today to support each party in continuing to promote and foster forward expansive healthy growth of the wellness and prevention model relative to dogs' health—as a first step, rather than promoting the older traditional drug-based models. This parallels the current human medical industry, which is also evolving right now and putting greater emphasis on the prevention or reversal of diseases and sickness.

My dream is that all dogs in the world are their happiest, healthiest, most joyful version of themselves. I want them to live as they were intended to live and be protected by the owners and industries they depend on. Finally, I want to see dog owners empowered with the knowledge and confidence to do their best for their dogs!

There's no greater gift you can give your dog or cat than the priceless gift of true health. Dogs are beautiful beings of love and light, which God placed on our planet for us to enjoy and love and, in most cases, for them to show us what matters most in life. After all, dog is God spelled backwards. In return, we can promote and be devoted to helping our dogs live their best possible lives.

FROM THE AUTHOR

AS YOU READ, KNOW THAT I AM NOT writing or speaking against any industry or profession. I often clarify roles of professions to align positive expectations and to explain what each profession covers and how it can heal or work with certain needs, as well as the limits of the profession in healing your pet. I'm not going to paint a picture of good and evil. As we progress as a society, new research is created and discovered. New learning takes place, and our collective knowledge grows. It's not a perfect world, nor will it ever be. However, when it comes to our pets' health, we are not victims. Additionally, I'm not claiming any industry is the villain. I do hold to the fact that pet owners rarely see or learn of the full story. I value truth and honesty. You do too. That's why you're reading this book.

The commercialized pet industry and traditional veterinary industry need to level up. Yes, I know it's easier said than done. Still, they need to update to the latest information relative to dogs and cats. They need to go to the next level concerning the health and wellness of their products. Honesty, transparency, and clear communication are a must. Consumers need to know how products are created so they can make informed decisions. How can pet owners make smart decisions when they're not given full information? They simply can't.

The commercialized pet feed industry needs to hire people who know the information you will read in this book. They need to have formal training in pet health, wellness, nutrition, epigenetics and safety before creating commercialized pet feed products.

Traditional veterinarians can sometimes give advice concerning what dogs should eat, both short term and long term. To give this advice, I advocate for them having the proper credentials or knowledge to do so. At the very least, they should refer clients to professionals who hold such credentials if their only knowledge on nutrition is from the company's products, they carry in-house to treat disease states. The dog's best interest must always be considered first to restore health and wellness and to remove pain if it is present.

The curriculum for veterinarian training must teach the latest research from the last decade at minimum, especially around the topics of immunity and vaccination protocols. Soon-to-be veterinarians need to know about short-term and long-term toxicity from vaccinations. They need to understand the impact of "preventative" products they recommend, like heartworm and flea control medications. Pet owners should always receive complete honesty. If a treatment or product is not actually needed based on the dog's health at the time, and where the owner wants the dog to be, the vet needs to say so. Only then can a dog's health and wellness truly be optimized.

Ultimately, I want what most dog owners want. For every industry that can potentially impact a dog's health negatively, to place the dog's health, wellness, and potential pain before their bottom line. The best interest of each dog's health and wellness should be at the forefront and should be the driving factor of those decisions because that is where their clients believe and expect it to be at a minimum.

For the latest updates or to get in touch for consultations, reach out to me at:

Email: questions@catalystgroupsolutions.com
Dog Page: facebook.com/dogwellnesscoaching
Author Page: facebook.com/Stephanie-Krol-100230538923667
Website: wellnessandhealthnow.com/about-the-book
Pet products I use or peers use:
wellnessandhealthnow.com/pet-products/

CHAPTER 1

A Better Path to Pet Health

I HAVE A GREAT DOG. IN FACT, HE'S THE BEST DOG (okay, I might be biased). And while he's getting older, we have lots of quality life we want to live together. Some call him Winston, and he's a Jack Russell Terrier—I call him, my little "crazed-weasel." He's rambunctious, very smart, and has a great sense of humor when it comes to other dogs and people alike.

We both like to go for walks in the dog park and pick on the people not paying attention to their dogs. Winston likes to bark at them and wake them up. He's "talking," making a joke, and it's funny to watch people and their dogs' reactions. Most people laugh with him. Real dog people—*nice people*—smile and even get the joke. Their dogs usually do too. I can tell the not-so-nice people right away because a small percent of them seem to get offended. They give you this sour look and their inner person shines through when this spunky Jack Russell jokes with them by razzing them on. Winston and I both enjoy these types of fun and games.

So, when he began throwing up violently at the not-yet-old age of eleven, and I took him to the vet like any good pet owner, I was horrified with what they told me. It was 2:00 a.m., and I went to a specialty vet clinic near where I live in Illinois. It was one of the worst nights of my life! Winston had lost a little of his spring prior to his episode. *The perils of aging*, I thought. If you're familiar with Jack Russell Terriers in general, you'll know they come spring-loaded with lots of energy and enthusiasm, as they can bounce and jump pretty high for their smaller stature. My boy had a little fatty tumor on his right front leg, and it had started to affect our daily walks. He was also having trouble seeing in the dark, but I just thought these were natural signs of aging. That's what the vets said. After all, it catches up with all of us eventually, doesn't it? Or does it? In my early forties, I had thought the same for myself until I started learning about real health, wellness, and disease prevention. So, originally, I had thought that maybe age had cost him a little of his vertical leap, but Winston was a healthy dog—or so I thought.

At that vet visit (and at another where I sought a second opinion), they told me it was just aging, plus a lot more. My best friend was going to die. They told me he needed emergency surgery or his spleen would rupture and he would bleed out. But even if we did get the surgery, he only had three to four months, with or without it, but I needed to do the surgery this week and set it up right away, or, in their words, I was going to kill my dog. I was utterly devastated. I love my dog madly. I love animals, in general. I have always had a special connection with all animals, and I am *passionate* about them. Growing up, I wanted to be a horse vet, and from age five, I rode and jumped horses professionally. I've always had this strong emotional connection to animals—even more strongly than I do to most people.

So when I heard the diagnosis, it was a brutal blow and hit me too close to home. It broke my heart. I had already gone through a difficult health journey with my horse, who ended up dying unexpectedly in the end. There's something in me, maybe in a lot of us, that can make us give up our common sense when someone with "doctor" in their name tells us something, because they have the expertise and education in this field, right? They know more than us, right? As an educator and a person who highly values education and expert opinions, a Doctor of Education, myself, I was just as much a victim to this tendency as anyone—maybe even more so.

As these vets told me what was wrong with Winston and what they could do (or what I had to do to fix him), I simply knew inside that this was wrong. Something in me rebelled. They did not know the daily care, the best food, the filtered water, and how I didn't spray toxic chemicals on him or our lawn. So how does this make any sense? If you have ever been in a vet clinic late at night, faced with a daunting decision, you may know what it felt like. You feel pressure to do something, make the call, and help your dog. But what if the solutions the vet and the whole pet feed industry offer us aren't the answers your dog needs? Surgery wasn't going to restore my best friend to his former self; it would just be the next step in his slide toward the grave, putting off the inevitable a little longer.

I refused to accept this. I know a great deal about principles that can help coach humans and also help dogs—but I had never connected them with Winston before. I have helped hundreds of people create a healthier lifestyle and regain their vitality, and I became determined that I would do the same for my best furry friend.

What you are about to read in this book started right there in the vet office when I refused to accept their prognosis and decided to take my dog's health into my own hands. It's super scary, but when you refuse to let your dog go, you have to take big risks to get big rewards! My choices were the safest, least risky, and most focused on health, wellness, pain removal, and healing. Like I said, I am an educator and a researcher, and I have put all my decades of experience in research and examination, not to mention years of coaching humans into healthier lifestyles, and I applied this experience to my dog.

When I saw what it did for him, I became convinced that I needed to share it with the world. There are too many dogs out there right now who are suffering. They're itchy, inflamed, losing the bounce in their step, and prematurely aging. Every meal of overly processed, cleverly marketed commercial pet feed, every toxin we put into their systems and on them because it's convenient, and every so-called treatment, pill, or potion we give them can be stealing their health and shortening their years. That's not okay. You and I can do something about it—for our dogs.

Likely, you've seen some signs in your dog that bother you. Like my Winston, your pooch may have some allergy symptoms. Winston had lost all the hair on his belly, and it was pink and inflamed-looking. Maybe your dog's hair thins out at certain times of the year, or it thinned and has stayed thin. She may chew her paws, scratch a lot, or lick her backside—usually in the living room when you have company over. Your dog may have sores on his skin, hives, pustules that burst, impacted anal glands, and a host of other symptoms—the problems can be as varied as the pets. I doubt you would be reading this book if there was not something concerning you about your best furry friend. The question before you is the same one I faced. *What will you choose to do about it?*

I had tried many options. I consider myself a researcher, and when I "get the bit in my teeth," I can be relentless. I had tried everything I could think of to help my buddy—everything the vets and the pet feed industry told me should work. But it didn't. My best friend wasn't getting better; he was getting worse, and almost at the point of getting a body part cut out, which I was told was my very best option.

His illness culminated with him throwing up and us at the vet together at 2:00 a.m., but that is not where it started. And it certainly would not be where it ended. I am about to teach you what you can do for your dog, often through a simple change of diet, a return to common sense and the basics of health, that will give him the nutritious food dogs need to be their healthiest, best selves. I have now coached many pet owners in this method, and the results are overwhelming!

My journey with Winston wasn't overnight; this takes time. It took time for your dog to get to this point, and it will take time to get him healthy again. But, as I discovered, it is rarely too late, and much disease can be reversed. This plan is not the fountain of youth for your dog, but it is the next best thing.

When Winston started really responding after about a week on the dietary principles, I'm going to teach you in this book, I was astounded to see how much "aging" fell away, leaving him much more like his usual springy, crazed-weasel self. Within a couple of weeks, he had a lot of the bounce back in his step and was even overjumping the couch, he felt so good. Over time, I saw countless improvements. While I could see the difference within a week (this is not an unusual result when you begin to help your dog by feeding him what his body craves), I can *still* see continued improvement now, over eighteen months down the road. The milestones may not come daily or even weekly at this point, but every few weeks or so we feel like we can see him improve in some area.

All those signs of inflammation I mentioned. Gone! The hair grew back on his belly and the insides of his legs within maybe four months, and his coat filled in and got an inch longer in the normal longer areas, as he is a broken-coat dog. The pink skin we thought was natural faded to its proper brown and white, and all the rawness and chafing seemed to go away. His paws, once so itchy and stinky, no longer bothered him. He moved quicker, the spring back in his step, and his eyes regained their bright gleam. He even seemed to see better at night, started to see an ant on the carpet, and that fatty tumor started to slowly shrink. I was stunned to see weekly healing, and it let me know I was doing right by my boy.

I had tried so many other things for Winston. I would soak his paws in apple cider vinegar and Epsom salts. Nothing. I tried the expensive organic pet feed—the best stuff I could find. Little or no improvement. I tried every trick in the book, but it was like time and toxins were catching up to my little guy, culminating in that terrifying trip to the vet and the diagnosis they gave me. If any of this sounds like your experience as well, it is my desire for this book to bring you hope. You can do this! I will help you overcome any barriers you can think up as to why it won't work, because the fact is, your dog is worth it. You are a caring, loving, smart, and creative pet owner, and together, we're going to make this work. I know Winston won't live forever, but he can live the best life he can have, for the greatest number of years, and we can enjoy every moment together. It's true for your fur baby too. Get ready to learn what a true Species Appropriate Diet involves—your dog will love it, and that's the best thanks you could ever ask for. Seeing that joy and healing in your dog's face will let you know you're making the right choice!

Everyday people are embracing a holistic movement to create better and safer living for their pets and themselves. This caring yet scientific approach leads to a reduced need for harsh vaccination schedules and chemical treatments. The premise of this book is simply this: the healthier your dog, the more years you'll get to have her by your side to love and snuggle.

Our pets are always there for us no matter what, through the good and bad times. As responsible pet owners, it's time to educate ourselves so we can make their lives as happy, healthy, pain-free, and protected as possible. Their lives and health fully depend on us. We are their whole world. Plus, in a special way, they take care of us every day too.

While I cannot say if the pet industry is purposefully lying to you, I do know that in the United States, we are just as segmented with pet health and wellness as we are with human health and wellness. We know there is a specialist for each human body part. The same exists in the pet industry now. Whether the commercialized pet industry or the veterinary industry, each one embraces the research and philosophies that came before them. I would like to think we are all doing our best for the love of our pets. My hope is that you embrace that philosophy throughout this book.

I will share the latest content and research about the two industries I just mentioned. You'll see how they relate to the true health and wellness of your dog. I'll also share my experiences and how I saved my dog's life. Ultimately, you get to be the judge and jury. For the last couple of decades, I've been an educator. I take my experience and knowledge from the field of education and couple it with my experience in the pet industry. On top of that, I add more than two decades of experience in the dog and horse industries. I pulled together some of the best content and latest research for you from the most influential industries in your pet's health and wellness. I will share what I have found through research and experience to help you understand what true health really means for your dog.

I invite you to enjoy and devour this book, my labor of love. I painstakingly and thoughtfully put it all together so you can create a healthy, happy, and pain-free lifestyle for your dog or puppy. I know that has been the goal from the very beginning when you first brought him into your family. My hope is for you to extend that relationship for as long as possible, even if you are just starting out and even if they are not in their best health right now. At times, I'll weave in health tips for you as well. I do this because what is good for our dogs is often very good for us as well. Before you learn about a better path to pet health, there's something you should know first ...

The Most Common Path to Disease in Our Pets and How It's Affecting Your Dog

The commercialized pet feed industry excels at marketing its products. However, that does not necessarily mean those companies know or care about what's best for your dog's health and wellness. It also does not mean they know what contributes to the health and well-being of your dog.

The same holds true with standard traditional veterinary practices. These include prolonged annual vaccine schedules; flea, tick and heartworm treatments; and the prescription of unnecessary drugs and antibiotics. With antibiotics, it's very much like in the traditional medicine world of humans. We call it healthcare and health insurance. It is sick care and sick insurance, unfortunately. As such, it is mislabeled, exactly like the health and wellness standards for pet care. It's important for me to mention again that this book is not against the veterinarians or the pet industry. At the same time, I believe it's important for you to know the whole story. For example, let me tell you about markups on some medications. According to the 10th edition of the Veterinary Fee Reference by the American Animal Hospital Association (AAHA), prescription drugs have markups of 113%, while heartworm preventatives and flea/tick products have markups of 76% and 65%, respectively (Myers, 2020). The May 2018 Veterinary Team Brief PDF discloses that heartworm preventive fees have a 90% markup. The standard protocols of traditional veterinary therapies are as commercialized as the pet feed industry. In fact, those two industries feed upon each other's standard for marketing procedures ... and it's taking a toll on your dog's health and wellness and, quite frankly, your bank account too. You think you're loving your pet and being the best owner ever by taking your dog to the vet for those annual vaccinations. However, I will explain later how those vaccinations truly contribute to overall toxicity, especially in terms of over-vaccination. You will also learn how to discover if your pet has immunity before it's suggested that you over-vaccinate your beloved pet.

Convenience Versus Health

Serving your dog pet feed products such as kibble, or any commercialized pet feed, for that matter, is totally convenient. Open the bag, pour kibble in the bowl, and mealtime's over, right? Easy peasy!

The problem is feeding your dog centers around your convenience instead of your dog's health. Shouldn't we take more than a couple minutes to dump a cup, glob, or freeze-dried food into a bowl? Absolutely. We show love to our pets through feeding them healthy and nutritious meals.

It is essential for dog owners who are committed to optimizing their dogs' health to ask smart questions:

- Is it healthy?
- Is this real food?
- Is it free from hazardous chemicals?
- Is it toxin-free?
- Does this food make my dog sick?
- Does what I'm feeding my dog contribute to disease?
- What's the cumulative effect of these foods on my dog's health?
- Am I truly loving my dog by what I'm feeding him?
- Am I showing care and love to my dog with what I put on his or her body, and what they absorb through their paws and skin?
- Am I aware and paying attention to what I put in my dog?
- Am I aware of fertilizers in my backyard and potential runoff?
- Am I aware of other people's backyards on dog walks and the chemicals they put on their yards, so I wash my dog's feet off after dog walks to prevent absorption of those toxins?
- Am I using toxin-free shampoo? Flea treatments? Heartworm preventative?
- Am I not over-vaccinating my dog with toxic chemicals?
- Am I aware of what's in vaccinations, drugs, flea chemicals, and preventatives?

Let's get back to the topic of the pet feed industry. The promises made on the packages of commercialized pet feed are often exaggerated as a puffery of sorts and outright inaccurate—or both. The bulk of the product often comes from nutritionally empty and worthless byproducts sourced from ground-up body parts, and not the nutrient-rich parts, unfortunately. These grotesque body parts could include beaks, ears, snouts, hooves, and whatever else falls to the floor during the rendering process in food production for human beings.

Meat packing companies make billions of dollars sending slaughterhouse waste to the pet feed industry. Some of the animal byproducts contain tumors, lots of fat, and other compromised forms of tissue. These byproducts are then milled with grains or compacted into materials dogs clearly do not need to eat. The quality of ingredients is so low that it barely qualifies as food for any living thing! Yet, hundreds of thousands of pet owners feed their animals those types of products on a daily basis. These items are in the majority of commercialized pet feeds of all kinds. This includes kibble, canned, freeze-dried, raw, and organic pet feeds.

Complicating the matter, many of these ingredients have zero nutritional value. They stress and damage your dog's digestive tract, cause allergies due to mixing plant foods with meat and the large amounts of fat, generate eating problems, and make your dog feel or become sick from an imbalanced gut. These issues commonly produce diarrhea, throwing up, inflammation showing up through allergies, and lead to serious health problems such as heart disease or cancer. The mixing of toxic synthetic supplements and fat creates even more complications.

The beneficiaries of all these problems are veterinarians, who, in turn, prescribe medicines such as antibiotics. Vets are not in the business of restoring health. It really isn't in their job description.

Health-restoration endeavors are left to holistic and Chinese medicine vets, or pet nutritionists.

As a loving and caring pet owner, I'm sure you have taken your pet to the vet at one time or another because something was off. I'm guessing your pet was prescribed a medication first. This medication probably made them sicker, or perhaps you came to realize that it would not work in the long term. Next, you went back to the vet, who wanted to put your dog on an antibiotic. Sometimes the first antibiotic does not work, even after your dog has been on it for a few weeks. Then, the vet puts your dog on another antibiotic. Still, after taking the recommended number of pills, your dog isn't himself or herself and seems ill. They had my dog on an antibiotic for two weeks. Then they did blood work for another two weeks. It was insane. It gets exhausting and expensive fast, doesn't it?

Did you know what the most common answer is to most issues that vets are unsure about? It comes down to giving your dog medication. These medicines create toxicity in your dog. They can disturb his or her natural immunity. They even create toxicity that the body stores in tumors, to tuck them safely away from organs to preserve health, other health conditions, and reduce inflammation. That's simply how living organs preserve life. Did you also happen to know that inflammation presents itself in many ways? It is the first dangerous step to cancer creation. We will get to that a little later.

To summarize, there are vicious health cycles that I want to help you break. If your dog is currently suffering, it's quite plausible you can restore your dog's health and wellness, prevent further deterioration, and save his or her life! That's the difficult situation I was in with my dog a year ago. I loved him and devotedly took him to the vet for twelve years. I thought I was showing my love by being the best pet owner possible. I even fed him the most expensive organic commercialized dog feed and supplements on the market. I did titer testing. I never placed chemicals on his body or in the backyard.

Unfortunately, and sadly, all of that was not sufficient! I had to find a way to save his life. You see, he was up for a splenectomy that was internally biopsied. My dog is very sensitive and needy. He would not have been a good candidate for what the vet recommended. I was told that with or without the surgery, my precious dog had only three to four months to live! Talk about heartbreaking news. I did not accept it. It was not good enough for me. Even with the most professional diagnostics from the best veterinary university and specialty clinic, I was still not convinced they had provided me with the answers I needed to decide on surgery or not.

Now you see why this book and its content are so very personal and why I want to share them with you. The purpose of this book is to educate pet owners like you who love their dogs and want to provide the best life for them. It was written to provide eye-opening content to help you arrive at true health restoration and wellness for your dog.

In my quest to save my dog's life, I was so blessed to learn and uncover invaluable information. I devoured multiple types of information from a wide array of sources in veterinary research and discipline. I spoke to the best of the best. I paid for a variety of consultations from experts to save my dog. My goal with this book is to give you everything I discovered so you can take exact steps to restore your dog's health and prevent diseases from getting a foothold. If you want to optimize your dog's health, reverse disease states, and bring up your puppy healthy, keep reading.

Breaking the Cycle Is Faster and Easier Than You Think

If I share with you that it is remarkably easy to replace commercialized dog products with the food you typically have around the home every day, would you, do it?

Would you take the time to learn a little bit about health and nutrition for your dog, given what you're reading here? I believe the answer is yes, given you purchased my book. I know you are clearly looking for better ways. You're not looking for information overload. You want real-world advice broken down in a step-by-step way you can process, understand, and implement.

What if I told you the cost of making the feeding transition was similar to your daily meal prep and at times even cheaper than spending $15 to $50 on a bag of kibble? How does that sound?

That's exactly what I'm talking about here! I'm not advocating that you take part in some science experiment in which you act like a chemist or doctor, mixing up meals for your pet. You're more like the chef! Your dog is your patron. And get this: it's fun and easy! We are talking about real and actual food, which can be regular or organic, that fits your dog's unique body and digestive system. This will allow your dog to feel healthy and energetic without tummy trouble or the creation of allergies or inflammation. Your dog will have energy, be happy, and have a beautiful coat and healthy teeth, simply from implementing this way of feeding. It may even create a new way to observe and connect with your dog, like it did for me.

Think of your normal kitchen like a local diner where your customers come in for food during the day. That's all you must do to break the cycle of serving up commercialized dog feed. You can connect with your dog by observation and by creating your own language. This will allow you to immediately tell if there is a real problem or something you can totally handle through diet. That cycle is often the source of our pets' health problems, along with vaccinations, drugs and topical chemicals put on our pets, or chemicals that are in our backyards. We will address those in detail later in the book.

What the Research Says

To help you understand the urgency of serving your pet better food and to show you how to avoid unnecessary and expensive trips to the veterinarian, I will share research about the harmful effects of commercialized dog feed and why it is not good for your pet.

Investigations on the source and effects of highly processed commercial pet feeds have produced valuable insights into the damage they cause. One tactic used by pet feed manufacturers to portray and sell their products as a healthy alternative is to pack the food with vitamins and other food-based supplements. Why? So they can present their product as essential and nutritionally "complete." They present it as important and vital to your dog's health; however, there is no guarantee those supplements are either healthy or beneficial for your dog. I will explain later why they are not.

Did you know each item of actual food (fruit, vegetable, meat) you eat or feed to your pet has the exact perfect amount of nutrients for that item and the perfect amount of nutrients for absorption of the vitamins in that food item? It's remarkable! It's almost impossible not to have complete nutrition with a varied, nutrient-dense diet.

We all need nutrients to stay healthy. These essential compounds found in food are necessary for maintaining a healthy life. These compounds provide energy, act as building blocks for growth and repair, and play a crucial role in regulating chemical processes (Australian Government Department of Health, 2013). Due to soil erosion and the lack of crop rotation, our soil is less nutrient-dense.

Many of us prefer eating organic food so we avoid GMOs and pesticides; however, a dog can do very well on non-organic food. When trying to reverse disease though, it's a better choice to use organic food, which has fewer toxic chemicals, and to remove any and all chemicals everywhere that can be placed on and in the pet you're trying to heal, and quite frankly, to prevent disease and toxicity.

The bold print on pet feed packages often reads like this: "All the vitamins your pet needs to stay healthy!" Words like those are exceptionally deceptive. It is very convincing marketing by an industry that must be fairly talented to make toxically baked, synthetic supplements and high fat content sound like an awesomely healthy combination. In essence, they are working the sales side of their business well, but is it done in an honest and ethical manner? I'll leave that for you to decide!

Feeding commercialized pet feed full of synthetic supplements or vitamins naturally occurring at excessive levels at one time, can be detrimental and toxic to a dog's health. Earlier, we learned how drugs create toxicity and how that toxicity is stored in tumors. The tumors are created by the body to preserve life. This is not a healthy way to preserve life or reverse disease in our pets.

Think about it. The addition of supplements in dog feed is an admission by pet feed manufacturers that the original product lacks real nutritional value. Otherwise, they would not add them as it costs money coming off their bottom line. Injecting food additives or supplements into dog feed is like coating a hotdog with a synthetic layer of Vitamin E and claiming it is a super-healthy product to eat. The hotdog may deliver a form of Vitamin E into the body, but the beneficial effects are speculative, at best, because the nutrient is so out of context with the food source. You also must consider whether it is a whole food source with nutrients, like in a vegetable or piece of fruit or meat.

The outcome of consuming nutritional substances out of context with their actual food origins creates a dietary shock that stresses the body instead of nourishing it. It would make derivative supplements like these worthless, but they also cause animals to grow lethargic or sick from continually trying to digest materials and chemicals their bodies are ill-equipped to handle.

Nutrients that work in synergy can come from natural food sources, regardless of whether they are organic or not. In a reprinted article titled "Fundamentals of Feeding" published in Dr. Shelton's Hygienic Review in June 1978, Ian Fowler explains that the consumption of concentrated items can produce an unexpected surge of nutrients. This can leave the body feeling depleted, weak and fatigued (Cinque, n.d.).

If our dogs' bodies can't detox all of these derivative chemicals, isolated nutrients, and all the excessive fat content being crammed into their systems from the commercialized pet feed industry, then their bodies go into an action of preservation by trying to save the vital organs, by creating tumors in a dog's body to hold toxins away from his or her vital organs so the body can maintain homeostasis and survive. This happens in humans too. The dog's body is trying to preserve and protect itself from death. The tumors serve to keep the dog alive, by isolating toxins like heavy metals, chemicals from vaccinations and otherwise inside of the tumor/s and safely away from vital organs.

The Down-to-Earth View and What We Intuitively Know

Let's get down to common sense. These same researchers admit that even feeding whole, natural food to dogs produces a form of stress in a dog's body. The type of stress is what one researcher calls "nutritional intensity."

Eating any type of food requires a certain amount of energy to break it all down. As you know, this process is called digestion. The point is digestion takes energy, which is why I recommend implementing the diet you'll read about later in this book. It takes the energy of the body at specific times and creates health and wellness. What the pet feed industry markets and sells is a type of concentrated pseudo-nutrition. Let's consider wolves, the closest relatives and ancestors of dogs.

Throughout the book, I will be referencing wolves from time to time because wolves and dogs share 99.9% of their DNA (Kasprak, 2016). Wolves eating in the wild did not eat pseudo-feeds or anything close. Out in Mother Nature, wolves always eat the organs first. Why? That's where the most dense nutrition is found. Wolves eat in a very digestion-friendly way.

Allow me to pull the curtain back further. Your body and your dog's body's largest expenditure of energy is digestion. Digestion creates free radicals in both pets and in humans.

Free radicals are atoms that can cause damage not only to cells and proteins, but also to DNA. Their accumulation has been linked to human diseases like cancer, and may play a factor in the aging process (Eske, 2019).

What's being digested? It obviously depends on what is eaten. Synthetic nutrients or otherwise always overload the system. As you know, almost all commercialized pet feed has synthetic supplements, and we have determined they are toxic. Sometimes the issue for digestion is that there is an overload of nutrients the body cannot process. This means the dog consumes fats, proteins, and carbs at once, along with supplements packed in. This act of feeding literally creates a dumping ground in your dog's stomach, which only has one chamber. One chamber means it can only digest one food type or item at a time. Placing a mix of fat, synthetic supplements, plants, fruits, and meats can only create toxicity in our dogs. If you look at nearly every commercialized pet feed, they include that mix. When you add the high fat content, they all create toxicity.

I am sure you have heard of detoxing. Over time, a number of bad items start to build up inside of your body. If left to their own devices, they can create toxicity. Whether it's your body or your dog's, it will take you down a bad path. The power and beauty of a detox is that it gives a body time to heal. Having only water for twenty-four hours flushes toxins out of a body in a healthy, natural way. This is in stark contrast to taking supplements for a detox (which is done for many human detoxes). Without a fast, a body never has a break or a reprieve from digesting, so it's not detoxing.

Ideally, with a dog's stomach, plants never touch meat and meat never touches plants (vegetables and fruits). The combination of those creates toxicity in a one-chambered-stomach animal. More on that later. Stay tuned.

If commercialized pet feed is not healthy, you may be asking yourself this question: Why does my dog devour it? That's a great question. Here's the answer: Deception by smell is a powerful tool used by the commercialized pet feed industry. A hungry pet or person responds to the smell of food chemically treated to appeal to his olfactory senses (this is the same with anything in a box you find at a store). The result is that a dog may be immediately stimulated by eating the synthesized chemicals, commercial foods, and highly marketed dog feed. However, as the food enters his body, it is hardly recognizable due to the dog's digestive system and makeup. Neither pets nor humans were made for daily negative chemical consumption. It's also not recognized in the normal chemical and biological processes involved in the breakdown of food into nutrients. The critical nutrients dogs need each day from their food fuel muscles, produce energy, and satisfy the feeding instincts of hungry animals.

When it comes out the other end, things get even worse. No doubt, you know exactly what I'm talking about. The amount of poo generated by dogs fed with commercialized kibble, canned food, or raw food is often three times as much compared to an animal being fed real meat, fruit, and vegetables that are suited for their natural dietary needs.

Rather than feeding your dog a pie-in-the-sky, supercharged commercial diet injected with synthetic supplements and vitamins, it is time to bring your dog's diet back down to earth. Just think about how wolves eat. They are very perceptive and wisely in tune with nature and their bodies. Eating how they ate can truly create health for our pets.

It's time to use common sense and a conscious approach that is scientifically based on what we know about dogs, their wolf ancestors, and the fact that dogs have a one-chamber stomach. More on this soon.

The Power and Benefits of Common Sense

Canines evolved from their wolf ancestors as opportunistic feeders, otherwise known as pack feeders. They learned through experimentation how to find food or hunt it down on their own.

As a result, dogs will generally consume whatever they find in front of them. This is what makes them forage things in the yard. The exception to dogs consuming almost anything is this: They usually (but not always) will avoid food if it is either 1) unsatisfying or 2) doesn't make them feel good. Dogs are smart that way. They will often turn up their noses at foods that don't suit them. That's what their instincts tell them to do.

The commercialized pet feed industry is highly skilled at tricking dogs. Their products make dogs think that the food smells or looks the part of real food. However, the dog's body later resists the deception. That's when pets either get sick directly or start building toxins that evolve into other disease states from eating fake foods that stress the body. These fake foods consistently fail the nutritional needs of a pet, regardless of his or her age.

The only way to counter these ill effects is to replace the fake foods in a dog's diet with real foods that meet their nutritional requirements. This means shifting from a menu that features highly processed foods packed with fake supplements to a menu with nutrients that can be absorbed in a far more healthy and natural fashion. This menu's food list can be easily broken down for fuel for the body, as opposed to waste and toxicity. These include raw and high-fiber foods that pet owners simply won't find at a retail pet store.

Perhaps you've heard that the healthiest way to feed your own body is to shop the perimeter of the grocery store. That's where real foods such as vegetables, fruits, and meats occupy the shelves and stands.

It's best to avoid buying your food from boxes, cans, and other highly processed sources. Shopping the perimeter is the best and usually easiest way for people to know what they're putting inside their bodies. It's likely a better choice for health and wellness.

The same holds true in food shopping for your dog. You and I cannot control what's inside pet feed products. Many times, we see words we do not recognize, let alone can't even pronounce! Words like Butylated Hydroxytoluene don't exactly sound digestion-friendly, do they? Quality control and setting the foundation for optimized health come into play when you assume the role of chef for your dog. Only then can you control the quality, content, fat, and what you, alone, place into the diet.

TIP 1

Although you will read more insights later, here are a few tips:

- The cleaner the diet, the more healing can take place.

- Be as chemical-free as possible.

- Only buy products when you know the exact process that the food went through to be created and sold. This is oftentimes much easier to do if you buy from local farmers who aren't commercialized and who care about the quality of what they're creating because their families eat it too.

Even Thomas Edison, who wasn't only known for creating the first incandescent light bulb in 1879, had predictions when considering the future of health and wellness in that doctors will not only prescribe medicine but also encourage their patients to take care of their body, pay attention to their diet, and understand the reasons and ways to prevent diseases (Buckenmaier III, C., 2018, Edison, T. A., 1847-1931).

Teamwork and Strength

The healthier you feed your dog, the more your precious pet will be happily and lovingly by your side for years to come. However, with convenience generally dictating what dogs are fed, it's easy to see that pet owners are required to shift their feeding habits if they want the absolute best for themselves and their dogs. The quality of your dog's life comes down to the quality of information you as a dog owner learn, along with the best practices you implement.

Recall that most of the time, a traditional veterinarian has not had one nutrition course. Getting advice from a traditional vet at times is not the best move if you want to facilitate healing, health, and wellness for your dog. However, if a dog needs surgery, has ingested poison, or has an emergency like a physical accident, then you would definitely seek out a traditional vet. The same goes for people who experience similar circumstances. We would immediately go to a traditional doctor.

People who want annual bloodwork or to dramatically increase their overall health and wellness should go to a holistic practice or practitioner or seek out naturopaths, nutritionists, osteopathic doctors, functional medicine doctors and coaches, and health and wellness coaches. When someone wants to create a health and wellness plan or a preventative plan for their dog, I recommend seeking out holistic vets, pet nutritionists, and pet coaches with holistic training. If you had a digestion or other gut issue, you'd go to a specialist such as a functional medicine doctor, coach, naturopath, or osteopathic doctor. Many times, for specific issues, a traditional doctor is not the ideal decision. Most of the time, they have not been trained in nutrition. Sadly, many doctors live very unhealthy lifestyles. Healthy and sustainable change comes down to which experts you go to for your information.

Currently, there are holistic vets who serve to improve our pets' lives. The golden guideline is to always do your research by reading reviews, asking clientele, and so on.

Additionally, you're always welcome to reach out to me for pet health and wellness coaching. I also assist individuals through patient advocate help, functional medicine coaching, and health and wellness coaching. If I cannot support your needs, I can always assist with referring you to someone from a huge database of highly trusted health and wellness practitioners. If you need help with pet diet implementation, choosing food items, or how to follow through with the process this book outlines, I am available for those consultations as well. As you can probably tell, pet health and wellness are my greatest passion! You probably already think of yourself and your dog as a team. I invite you to take it up a notch. Become each other's health advocates. This special form of teamwork produces a lifelong bond. For your dog, it is formed around a healthy diet, which creates and facilitates preventative medicine.

Once a pet owner leads his or her dog to a better lifestyle, those annual vet visits take on a different tone and direction. While some vaccinations like rabies are required by law, the layers of vaccinations recommended by many vets are unnecessary. The truth is that there are wonderful alternatives for situations like boarding, and you don't need to over-vaccinate your dog just to provide proof of health.

In fact, we have been learning that vaccinations have less to do with health and more to do with toxicity. There are other ways to provide immunity, like titers (or titer testing), which provide immunity rather than proof of vaccination. However, it's always best to get a dog-sitter rather than board at a facility that requires you to get unnecessary vaccinations. This is especially important if they won't take proof of titer. Want to love your pet? Don't trade your pet's health for a vacation.

A healthy dog fed with good nutrition develops an immune system strong enough to protect them from threats that the pet industry loves to treat. Unfortunately, that industry also scares us into unnecessary treatments. I experienced those directly with my dog, including unbelievably expensive medicines, chemicals, and sometimes unnecessary surgeries.

In some cases, the treatment is far worse than the condition it is supposed to cure! For example, flea and tick applications physically poison your pet to combat infestation or attachment. A healthy dog doesn't get anywhere near the number of fleas or ticks you'd think he or she would get when you're hiking or doing other outside activities. Sometimes it's the simple items that work wonders, like a $3 flea comb in this scenario. I maybe see one or two fleas on my dog per year, if at all!

Concerning ticks, I have never had any tick problems with any of my previous dogs. With my current dog, I have only had one situation. It happened because he and I went off the designated path in a forest preserve. Live and learn! However, in over forty years of owning dogs and over thirty years of owning horses, I have only had one tick situation. Granted, there are variables, such as where you live. Still, healthy dogs are much less bothered by bugs internally and externally. Their healthy internal terrains show outward in their shiny, sparkly eyes and coats. Both humans and dogs must be healthy internally to be healthy externally.

I encourage you to take a few moments now to consider what you truly want for your pet. You are the family member upon whom they depend for every aspect of their health and life conditions. You are their whole world.

Moving from a byproduct-based, commercialized kibble, canned, raw, or rehydrated food menu to a health-and-wellness-based program does require a bit of motivation. Following this plan means you decide what is important for your dog's health, wellness, and nutrition. However, you now have a much clearer introduction as to what it looks like, and soon I'll cover the steps to make that happen. You have learned so much thus far about the products sold by commercial pet feed companies and how they are not what you want to feed your beloved pet. This book will provide a step-by-step approach and help you transition to a better and healthier life for your dog. I'll also share tips that apply to people when it connects to the topic at hand. You'll see just how much you and your dog are connected.

In our next chapter, we'll address more concerns and practical solutions.

CHAPTER 2

What the Pet Industry Doesn't Want You to Know

YOU LOVE YOUR DOG. Don't we all?! Given the fact we love our dogs so much, it can be a bitter pill to swallow when we learn the truth about the pet industry. You can probably already guess. The goal of the pet feed industry is profit. Sure, they wrap up their food products in cute, heartwarming commercials and use gorgeous artwork on every product sold. Yet, at the end of the day, each company is looking at one thing: its bottom line. To be fair, this is exactly what every company does. It's just that the great companies do it ethically and honestly. What you do going forward with the knowledge you will gain here will truly make a difference.

Pet lovers are the consumers, and they're the ones getting tricked, along with their dogs. They think they're giving their dogs nutritious food when they're not. The food is designed to be as appealing to the dog as possible, while being made as cheaply as possible. Owners are being sold a bill of goods on the marketing and on the bags, boxes, cans, etc. It's very upsetting to find out that you did what you thought was solid research on the best products, foods, supplements, and care ... trusting those who you thought had your dog's best interests in mind, only to find that they were speculating and guessing, giving a generic answer to get the next patient in the door, or basing their answer exclusively on their bottom line. Or it was simply their lack of knowledge. You trusted these folks to help you make the best choices for your dog because you love your dog and you want to give him the best care possible. You took her to the most revered and recommended vets in your area, or so you thought.

Through it all, now you're learning about the reality of trusting those so-called experts who are in charge. Now, you have decided to take charge yourself. Why? Because no one loves your dog more than you do! When faced with the facts, you know that you are just as capable and brilliant to make the best decisions for your dog as they are. I hope this book empowers you to take charge of your dog's care, starting today. I'm inviting you to call the shots and ask the questions needed from an educated standpoint as you continue reading. What you learn and implement can truly impact your dog's life, as well as your own. Your dog will start moving toward true health and wellness. We all must start somewhere, and we can do that by gaining new knowledge and applying it so we do our best going forward ... both for ourselves and for our dogs.

Here's a new bottom line I'd like to share with you. (Hint: It doesn't focus on profit!) If you love your dog, you're not going to feed him or her commercialized food that will diminish their quality of life, shorten their time on earth with you, or, most tragically, cause them to die an early death.

You show your dog love by the quality of food you're feeding him. Let's lay out a few steps to start with, and let's start from the beginning.

What's in Commercialized Pet Feed (Kibble, Canned, Freeze-Dried, and Combinations)? Are All Commercialized Foods Unhealthy?

If the commercialized pet feed that most dog owners are buying and feeding their dogs is not healthy or even nutritious, why is that?

First, here are the four categories of pet feed (in no order), in case you want more information on this topic:

- kibble
- canned
- freeze-dried
- any combination of the above

Here's what is happening behind the scenes. (You can bet you'll never see commercials sharing these facts.) In the process of mass-producing food for human consumption, there are countless byproducts. Why? Because humans are not going to eat certain parts that aren't good for us, but they aren't good for our dogs either.

Even dogs in the wild don't eat waste products or fat. These byproducts are pure waste.

What's included in the waste? It could be any combination of the following:

- tumors
- organs
- bones
- eyes
- ears
- hooves
- cartilage
- fat
- and more

You're right. It is a disgusting list. What's more disgusting and scarier is that these byproducts are going into a wide array of pet feed brands being sold today, in aisles you and I walk down every week.

Companies producing food for humans are faced with a dilemma. What do they do with all that waste? As you can guess, disposing of the waste in an eco-friendly, ethical way can be costly and takes away from their bottom line. They wanted to find a cheaper solution and, even more exciting, one that makes them money. And they did.

This is where the pet feed industry comes in. They become the recipient of all the byproducts humans will not or cannot eat. For these two profit-focused industries, this is a massive win/win. One industry's waste becomes another industry's raw materials for products, which, in this case, is pet feed. Kind of scary, right? When it comes to you and your dog, it's anything but win/win.

You may be thinking, "Okay. Wait a minute. Are you saying that all commercialized pet feeds are bad and unhealthy?" Based on my extensive research and experience with animals, my answer is "Yes. Absolutely." That is my answer in light of any one of the earlier reasons you read about, which included synthetic supplements; mixing fruits, vegetables, and meats; excessive fat; the use of byproducts; and other items dogs don't eat even in the wild.

What perpetuates the problem is that pet feed consumers are not aware of the reality of what is happening, neither from the point of view of looking at the industries nor from the point of view of what's going into your dog's food bowl. Instead of awareness, you and I as consumers are constantly and strategically bombarded with nonstop, highly customized marketing tactics rather than truth in marketing and ethics of quality.

You might recall the popular trend that focused on grain-free pet feed. This trend was deceptive, and many dog and cat owners fell for it. For years, dog feed included grains. Grains were included to boost profit because grains are cheaper than meat. What's the plot twist? Grains should never have been included in the first place! At some point, pet feed companies created grain-free versions and then relaunched large marketing campaigns, which, of course, framed them in a way that made them sound like they actually care for your dog.

The new marketing push was that dogs are basically wolves, which are mostly carnivores. This is actually true. Following that line of thinking leads to the idea that you must not feed your dog grains.

Ultimately, the theory suggesting grain was necessary was a flawed and inaccurate mess. The problem is that the pet feed industry replaced grains with cheap pseudo-food. The absence of grain in commercialized pet feed did not equal the addition of something healthy; this just created another marketing ploy. Uninformed dog owners were left scratching their heads, wondering what was making their beloved pooches ill.

The word kibble gets tossed around a lot. What is kibble exactly? Besides the fact that it's dry food, what else do we know about it? You may be surprised.

The production of dry dog food kibble involves combining and processing the ingredients used to make the feed before being cooked, which must meet the nutritional requirements of dogs and be balanced (Scott, 2017).

Once you expose your dog's kibble to air, the oxidation process begins, causing rapid changes that can be harmful if not managed carefully. With each opening, the risk of health problems can increase, especially for the fats and oils in the kibble that are highly susceptible to oxidation (Scott, 2017).

Studies suggest that the ingestion of rancid fats can lead to the destruction of vitamins (Lease et al., 1938) (Pavcek & Shull, 1953).

Rancid fats have been associated with a range of health problems, including nutritional deficiencies leading to poor health and growth, alopecia, gastrointestinal issues, and impaired liver and kidney function (Greenberg et al., 1953).

How Do Most of These Companies Make Their Commercialized Food?

It's a question all dog owners need to ask so they can learn to protect and truly care for the dogs they love. The pet feed industry usually seeks out the lowest grade and cheapest byproducts and supplements it can find to create their product.

Most companies create their pet feed by implementing a technique called rendering. Have you heard the term before? Rendering refers to the action of converting animal by-products and waste materials, including meat, bone, and fat, into pet feed. It can also be applied to non-animal products to break them down into pulp. During rendering, the material is dried, and the fat is separated from the bone and protein to produce a fat commodity and a protein meal. Despite its usefulness, the occupation of a renderer is often described as dirty and hazardous (Wikipedia, n.d.).

In a nutshell, these byproducts are not safe or healthy for humans to eat, and yet they're used in commercialized pet feed. From rendering, pet feed companies recreate the byproducts to smell enticing to dogs. As you know, dogs have a strong sense of smell. Surprisingly, though, they have a fairly weak sense of taste. This is why pet feed companies work hard to ensure their pet feed will smell tempting to our dogs, who are deceived into thinking what they're eating is worth eating ... when it's really not.

You've probably wondered about raw versus cooked. Now that you've discovered the truth about the pet feed industry, your brain may be working double-time to figure out a healthy solution, and fast. At this point, it may be crossing your mind to trash your commercial pet feed and decide to cook healthy, natural, and wholesome foods for your dog from your kitchen. (This is one reason why it's important to finish this book. It will give you the full story as well as strategies and recommended examples.) Feeding your dog what you believe to be good meals consisting of cooked human food is not a dog-friendly strategy. It can cause a level of toxicity from combining plant foods with meat. Toxicity can also come from supplements being added, excessive fat not being removed, and meat being cooked. Dogs are biologically designed to eat raw meat, offal, bone, plants and fruits. It's common for dogs to get sick when they eat cooked food. It can impact their health quickly (like diarrhea), harm them over time, or both—just like issues that can be caused by commercialized feed. Once again, this is where science comes in. Dogs have evolved from wolves and have gone on to adapt to their environments. You may be wondering what's healthiest for them. The answer: raw food. Science and research have proven this time and time again (The Darling Experiment Limited t/a Honey's Real Dog Food, NA, 25).

What's the problem with cooked foods for dogs? They seem healthy, right? They can be healthy for you as a human being, and there are many raw courses for people if you're interested. However, for most animals, it may surprise you that raw is best. Cooking foods, like veggies and meat, is not healthy for your dog. Cooking bones and meat diminishes their healthy properties and changes the structure of the bone. Bones can become devoid of nutrition. At times, they can become dangerous for dogs to eat. Why? Because once bones are cooked, they get weak. This can cause shards, fragments and slivers, causing potential obstructions. That's why you should never feed cooked bones.

Are Allergy Diets Real and Legit?

Spoiler alert: Allergy diets are mostly pointless. The reason is that allergy really means inflammation. As we've talked about, you cannot reverse a disease state unless you get to the cause. Allergies are symptoms of the real problem, which is inflammation. Then, you have to ask yourself what is driving the inflammation.

How does this come about? When vets (and many times, traditional doctors) come up against something they cannot quite figure out or diagnose with certainty, their general go-to response is "It's an allergy." This has grown into somewhat of a catch-all category. The problem is that the meaning of allergy varies. Although the issue is categorized as an allergy, there is still a lot of uncertainty around the fact that allergy causes inflammation, which is what kills humans and animals. It's easier to categorize diabetes or any other autoimmune disease, but it's the inflammation that is thrown out to the entire body that kills you. For example, it's the inflammation in someone's lungs from having pneumonia that can cause death.

Another issue is that many times, veterinarians will recommend a prescription drug for your dog to suppress the symptom. A common example is a drug to stop itching. At that point, it becomes possible that your dog is on some type of allergy med for the rest of her life! That opens further issues. What are the short-term side effects? What are the long-term side effects? Is the dosage recommended safe for your dog? Notice how the supposed cure in this scenario opens more questions and concerns. Don't forget you'll be paying for those meds every month too. It's another vicious cycle that, again, only creates more toxicity in your dog's body. It also creates more inflammation cascading through the first step of cancer creation.

Often, dogs are dealing with a type of inflammation or toxicity that is not being addressed or remedied. This starts with their first shots or commercialized dog feed or chemicals you may be placing on them. Inflammation is part of the detailed biological response from body tissues when they interact with harmful stimuli. These stimuli may include damaged cells, irritants, or pathogens. Interestingly enough, it's a protective response (like that of a tumor). The goal of inflammation is to eliminate the cause or source of the problem and start the process of repairing the tissue. When more and more toxicity is added to the body, it stops healing itself because it simply cannot keep up.

The issue is not so much what triggers the problem; the issue is the underlying foundation of inflammation and if it's allowed to continue for healing. For example, inflammation helps heal a surface problem, like a cut or an injury. That inflammation is perfectly needed and warranted. In fact, inflammation is what needs to be addressed to optimize your dog's immune response and overall health. The best way to remedy inflammation is not with meds or shots because they only create more toxicity and overburden the body. Remedying inflammation comes from the food you feed your dog. Remove the cause, and the body will heal. It's an amazing machine or organism (more on that later). There is always hope for healing if the body is unburdened and if the entity being healed has the time to eliminate toxicity.

When toxins from the food your dog eats are in his body or are created by the internal or external ways items enter the body, your dog's body must deal with those. This puts strain on the digestive system. Those toxins can also seep out through your dog's skin. This is problematic for hair follicles and skin tissue. Symptoms from toxins and inflammation can be countless. They can show up as hair loss, low energy, diarrhea and digestion issues, and anything that is not normal for your beloved pet.

When allergies appear, many pet owners start scanning their environment. They ask themselves, "What is triggering this reaction?" This is not bad, per se. It is important to know what your dog has access to.

However, it's an outside-in approach. When it comes to your dog's health and longevity, you'll get the best results implementing an inside-out approach. Thus, the focus of this book: what you feed your dog.

What About Raw Dehydrated Foods? Are They Okay?

No. Here's why. With foods that are dehydrated or freeze-dried, not only the water is removed. The removal also includes precious nutrients. In commercial pet feeds, this happens due to the way the items are dehydrated as well as how they are pasteurized, which uses a high-pressure pasteurization.

High Pressure Processing (HPP) is a non-thermal technique used for food preservation. Food products are placed in a special chamber filled with water and then subjected to high levels of specific pressure for a few minutes to a few hours. The pressure inactivates harmful microorganisms like bacteria and viruses that can cause food to spoil and make us sick (Krestel-Rickert, 2018).

Some companies insert bacteriophages, also known as phages. A bacteriophage is a virus that targets and infects bacteria. The term "bacteriophage" translates to "bacteria eater" since these viruses are capable of destroying their host cells (Scitable By Nature Education, 2014). Phages serve to further enhance the safety of the raw products. They are utilized by nature to keep bacterial balance, and have been doing so since ancient times. They are a natural, biological method of controlling harmful bacteria in unprocessed foods, which can make them safer to consume. Historically, phages have been vital for sustaining a balanced microbial environment. They are able to target and eliminate particular pathogens without affecting beneficial bacteria. (Iftikhar, 2019).

When the raw dehydrated food is rehydrated in the future, it is impossible for the food to return to its complete natural and most healthy state. Rehydrating food means your dog loses out on the full healing properties and co-nutrients contained in the food in its natural state. Compare the look and taste of a fresh mango to one that has been dehydrated. The difference in taste and texture is painfully obvious.

Many times, raw dehydrated pet foods are quite expensive. The unfortunate twist is that, often, dog owners believe because the price is high that this naturally means the quality of pet food is high. This is inaccurate. The other issue is that the pet feed industry often adds ingredients to raw dehydrated and freeze-dried pet feeds. Usually, these include ingredients to preserve the shelf life of the food and may include different types of oils, supplements, veggies, and so on, as mentioned previously. Most of the time, the fat content is also very high. Don't believe the hype that raw dehydrated dog feed is "as healthy as" or "as good as the real thing." It's not.

CHAPTER 3

Breaking Down Disease

THE GOAL IS TO KEEP OUR DOGS HEALTHY and alive for as long as possible because we love them madly, right? It's the least they deserve for all the love and affection they give us—as well as the love, affection, and protection we give them, keeping them happy, healthy, and pain-free. Reading this book is proof you are passionate about this and about giving your pet the best care. You're willing to learn and to do the work. In light of that, there are two main types of threats to our dogs' health that each dog owner must be aware of and face.

There are over two hundred documented diseases that can impact your dog's life (Pet Health Network, n.d.) (Clark, 2017). Systems that can be impacted include vascular, hormonal, digestive, musculoskeletal, neurological, reproductive, bony, and excretory. Areas that may be impacted include auditory, visual, and epidermis (Pet Health Network, n.d.) (Clark, 2017).

Ultimately, all of these diseases and disorders fall into one of two categories:

1. constructive
2. degenerative

Constructive diseases in humans are ones like flus, colds, measles, and the like. When hit with one of those diseases, the body instantly takes action to remove what is ailing it. Whatever is coming out of the body, mucus or otherwise, is a human body's attempt to rid itself of disease so it can return to its healthy state (Goldhamer, D.C., 2010) (Brown, 2019). In dogs, the most common constructive diseases are parvo and distemper. In those instances, a dog's body goes into emergency mode. Just like in humans, a dog's body is trying its best to remove waste and toxins because they are putting the dog's body in danger. Just like in humans, a dog's body is working to get itself back in harmony, internal balance, and health.

Degenerative diseases are characterized by degenerative cell changes. This affects tissues or organs and causes them to deteriorate over time. Depending on the diagnosis, the changes may include irreversible deterioration along with the loss of function in the organs or tissues. These are the types of disease states we are looking to reverse and prevent with this diet.

Dr. John Tilden was a prominent American physician and health science advocate. In the 1930s, he wrote Toxemia Explained. In that book, he identifies and shares the seven stages of all chronic diseases. The stages apply to all living organisms. I'll cover each one and share a few insights.

The stages can apply to all living organisms.

1. Enervation: Enervate means "to deprive of strength or vitality; weaken physically or mentally; debilitate" (Collins Dictionary, n.d.). During step one, a body hits a point where it becomes rundown. Consequently, it's no longer able to get rid of toxic byproducts. This produces an impairment. This leads to step two.
2. Toxicosis: This is "any disease or condition caused by poisoning" (Collins Dictionary, n.d.). A synonym for toxicosis is systemic poisoning. During this phase, toxins build up. The tissues and blood of a body grow packed with toxins that should have been eliminated but were not.
3. Irritation: Step three is when the toxins begin to irritate the body. A very low level of inflammation occurs. There are no major signs of disease, but vitality is nowhere near 100%. Minor health issues begin to show up because the toxins are obviously still living somewhere in the body. The irritation could include any variety of issues, from itchiness to negative feelings.

4. Inflammation: In this stage, inflammation is noticed. The person or dog is aware of the inflammation and any associated discomfort or pain. The body puts effort into coping with the inflammation in an attempt to cleanse and repair. This is the body's strongest attempt to resolve the inflammation.
5. Ulceration: Poisonous matters have started damaging tissues and cells in this stage. The body experiences pain, sometimes intense pain. It's possible the body will create an ulcer to contain the toxins in order to produce relief. The best-case scenario is that the ulcer is resolved (if the source of the issue is remedied). Otherwise, the body will enter the next stage.
6. Induration: Induration is the "hardening of a normally soft tissue or organ" (The Free Dictionary by Farlex, n.d.). This also includes scarring. In this phase, the body generates tumors or hardened tissues like scar tissue. The tumor quarantines the dangerous toxins. The body's flexibility usually diminishes at this point in the tumorous area. Surgery is usually recommended.
7. Cancer: In the final stage, the vitality of the body diminishes. Toxicity has raged on for too long. The brain no longer can control the cells. Cells are overwhelmed. Cancerous cells, which are parasitic, are present and start to greatly multiply. Tissues and organs can begin to die, leading to whole-body death.

Are Vaccinations Necessary for Immunity and Health?

As you're starting to see, a quality diet for your dog sets a foundation for optimal health. What your dog eats is either preventative care or disease-creating. There is no neutral ground. Every bite matters for humans and dogs.

People have healthcare. What's interesting about that word is that it's commonly used yet highly inaccurate. People truly have "sick care" as mentioned previously and expanded upon here. That's what it is—caring for the sick. However, when the focus is on science-based prevention, through what we put on and in our bodies as well as our dogs' bodies, the presence of sickness is likely to diminish or vanish.

What about vaccinations? In your dog, a vaccination cannot prevent disease or help your dog escape death. Vaccination does not equal immunity. Once again, vaccinations fall in the category of outside-in rather than inside-out. Long-term vaccinations can eventually deprive your dog of its strength and vigor and create toxicity. The goal is that your dog's body be in optimal health to overcome disease and detox symptoms from toxicity in the body. Meaning, your dog can fight off diseases itself to the furthest extent possible. Vaccinations can hinder and hurt your dog's natural life-giving state of being (Henriques, 2020) (Jordan, 2020).

What is alarming is that vaccinations can set the stage for degenerative diseases, allowing them to get a foothold in your dog's body, again, creating toxicity and then inflammation. The more toxins, the less healthy your pet will be. Vaccinations also cause wastes to stay inside of your dog's system—ones that would have regularly been booted out by your dog naturally through their urine, skin, eyes, ears, and feces.

Simply put, it is best to avoid vaccinations to the extent possible, but if you have a vaccinated pet, you can definitely detox them through this diet and return their health. I do realize that many states require rabies shots, as we talked about earlier.

Ronald Schultz, a professor at the School of Veterinary Medicine at the University of Wisconsin-Madison, has conducted research on vaccinations in dogs for several decades. His studies have shown that most annual vaccines are unnecessary because immunity can last a dog's lifetime. Excessive vaccination can pose a threat to a dog's well-being and survival, causing skin issues, allergic responses, and autoimmune disorders. Vaccines should only be administered to animals that face a considerable risk of infection. The Lyme disease and kennel cough vaccines, for example, are often unnecessary for household pets with limited contact with other dogs. Veterinarians should consider an individual dog's risk for developing a particular disease when recommending vaccines because vaccines carry a risk of causing notable harm. According to him, providing a vaccine that is not required poses an avoidable danger to the animal. The recommendation to limit the number of vaccines might be debatable, particularly for those veterinary clinics that rely on annual vaccinations to generate the greater amount of their revenue (Schultz, 2003). Recall that disease states can be relevant to toxemia levels, which can be caused by the vaccinations themselves due to the many toxic ingredients in them that we previously talked about.

When it comes to your dog's immunity, vitality, and health, put your trust in yourself, what you're learning here, and what you're feeding your dog. When you feed in this manner and learn to observe your dog, you will be able to note almost immediately what may be off. You'll know if it's a life-altering situation that needs a vet, a detoxing symptom, or simply their digestive system needing a short fast to fix what may be ailing them.

Has your vet shared this information with you?

- Pet vaccines contain toxic additives, such as aluminum, that can have harmful effects on animals. These substances can cause various side effects, including seizures, cancer, autoimmune diseases, asthma, diabetes, multiple sclerosis, arthritis, and even fatality (Saba, 2017).

- A recent study revealed a concerning link between aluminum in cat vaccines and cancer. The study suggests that the vaccine could increase the risk of cancer in about one in 1,000 cats. To minimize this risk, veterinarians tend to administer vaccines below the elbow or knee joint in the cat's leg since certain cats are prone to developing cancer at the vaccination site. This makes it easier to amputate the affected area if necessary (Saba, 2017).

- The dosage of vaccines for dogs and cats is standardized, regardless of their size or breed. This implies that there is no customization of vaccine dosage based on the animal's weight or other characteristics. Consequently, smaller dogs and cats are at a greater risk of experiencing vaccine damage due to the high dose relative to their body size (Dodds, 2017).

- Some veterinarians believe that the kennel cough vaccine for dogs is unnecessary. They argue that kennel cough is not as dangerous or contagious as it is often portrayed and is similar to a common cold in humans. Additionally, the vaccine may not be effective since there are more than 15 viral strains that can cause kennel cough, but the vaccine only protects against two of them (Dobbins, 2017).

When talking about vaccinations to your vet, the above topics are ones to consider discussing.

What Is a More Researched and Safer Option than Vaccinations That Can Still Prove Immunity?

When this question is asked, many times a topic called titer testing comes up. The term titer refers to the measurement of the concentration of an antibody in a sample by determining the highest degree of dilution at which the antibody can still produce the clumping (agglutination) of the corresponding antigen (Oxford University Press, n.d.).

What are titer tests exactly? The use of titer tests is a method that pet owners and veterinarians can employ to reduce the chances of both needless vaccinations and infectious diseases. A titer test is a blood test that measures the antibodies in the bloodstream and can inform you whether your dog's immune system is still protected by a previous vaccine or natural immunity. If the immune system is still active and producing antibodies, it may not be necessary to administer another vaccine at that time (Richmond MA, CPTD-KA, 2014, 2020).

In other words, titer testing for dogs is a type of blood test. The goal of a titer test is to determine whether your dog has enough antibodies to combat and defeat a particular disease. The cost commonly ranges between $40 to $200. At the end of the visit, you leave with the numbers (results) on a piece of paper.

If you research online, you'll see that titer testing is commonly framed as a "get out of vaccination card." At the end of the day, it's a great reason to have a titer test done on your dog if anyone is pressing a vaccination on your dog. If you have a specific circumstance or situation coming up that requires your dog to be vaccinated, a titer test can potentially help you gain access and entrance without adding toxicity to their body. This, of course, helps you bypass harmful and costly vaccinations. Essentially, that is the only reason to do a titer test. A titer test doesn't tell you if your dog can combat a disease. It tells the immunity level of the dog (and can also show immunity levels in people). Many believe that titers are a farce or sham. They believe one test like this can't show if you are immune or not, but that's exactly what it does show.

It is unnecessary to vaccinate animals that already have sufficient protection against a particular disease. To determine if an animal has enough immunity, a titer test can be performed. This ensures that vaccinations are given only when they are needed and not overused unnecessarily (Schultz, 2016.)

You should also know that dogs do have other kinds of immunity that aren't often studied. Have you heard of nasal immunity? Nasal immunity is a long-standing component of the mucosal immune system in vertebrates (National Center for Biotechnology Information, U.S. National Library of Medicine, 2014). In other words, nasal immunities protect our dogs long after a titer zeroes out and becomes obsolete. Dogs experience the world through their noses, as we all see on our fun dog walks.

The safest option for your dog's health and immunity is to carefully choose what you're feeding your dog. Dog nutrition has been heavily researched. It's the absolute best way to deny entry of toxins inside your dog's body and to set him up for optimal health. The only way to do this is for you to control the foods you purchase and how the meals are prepared.

What Is the Basis of This Book and the Concepts We Draw on for Healthy Dog Food?

The basis of this book is health science, which sets your dog up for optimal health and gives you many more years of joy, memories, love, and painless health and wellness with her. Health science is not yet a widely common phrase, but more and more people are realizing that one drug leads to another and leads to more sickness, toxicity, and disease. It is an offshoot of naturopathy. It relates to orthopathy, which is a philosophy of health and healing that emphasizes the importance of natural and non-invasive methods in restoring and maintaining health (Wikipedia, n.d.).

Health science is the discipline of applied science which deals with human and animal health (Health Science Journal, n.d.). There are two categories of health science:

1. The study, research, and knowledge of health (which is what you're doing now by reading this book)

2. The application of that knowledge to improve health, cure diseases, and increase our understanding of how humans and animals function (Science Daily, n.d.)

This lifestyle empowers dog owners like you to not only put an end to troubling symptoms, but also to put an end to your dog's experiences and help resolve diagnosed diseases that your dog has. This method is grounded in nature and science and helps dog owners create the absolute best lives possible for their dogs. Sound good and reasonable? If so, keep reading.

CHAPTER 4

Why are Certain Veterinarians Adverse to a Species Appropriate Diet?

DOES THE NARROW SCOPE of traditional veterinary medicine limit the understanding of health restoration in pets? Does it potentially create an unnecessary and negative bias against raw food? When you hear the phrase "raw food," you may be programmed to get nervous or worried because of something you read or perhaps something your vet or a friend told you. Maybe they heard about bones causing obstructions or about dogs getting shards in their throats. What about the bacteria in raw meat? My dog will get sick from E. coli and salmonella! I understand your concerns. We love our pets and are concerned for their safety and well-being. After all, you would not be reading this book and trying to find a better way if you weren't concerned and didn't truly care deeply for your pet.

In fact, I'm thrilled you are asking those questions. It only proves your love for your dog. It also shows your willingness to have an open mind and to learn and grow. That positive mentality equips you for real change that can save your dog's life or provide the healthiest way of life to prevent sickness and disease before they occur. Unfortunately, so many of us and our dogs are already sick. This was another point of motivation to write this book. The companies and people against raw feeding hold tightly to their argument. Why? Because it's effective at scaring dog owners away from using raw food, and sometimes they are misinformed or have only learned a little about it, and haven't taken the time to understand how it all really works and benefits our pets. So, as you can probably guess, there's much, much more to the story.

It's safe for your dog to eat raw foods. This is possible because your dog has stomach acid that is over ten times more potent than what us humans have. Just because raw food will make you sick does not mean it will make your dog sick. The bodies of dogs are created and designed to eat raw meat. Their systems can digest and dispose of the meat before putrefaction begins (Suzuki, 1987) (Wernimont et al., 2020).

Just so you know, putrefaction is the process of decay or rotting in a body or other organic matter. Dogs process food quickly. Humans do not. It may take a dog two to three hours to process fruits, five to six for vegetables, and twelve to twenty-four hours to process meats. Of course, it depends on the health of their digestive tracts. Are they healed from years of toxic kibble and drugs, or not? Digestion time can vary. However, those times are roughly for the average gut-healthy dog and what I have experienced with my own dog. While it may sound surprising and gross, dogs can eat and digest rotten flesh without problems. When humans eat raw flesh, putrefaction can occur. When it starts, it produces horrific toxins that can create multiple health issues in the person's body, not to mention all the bacteria we simply cannot digest in a healthy way.

If you hear vets, friends, or neighbors touting the dangers of raw food for dogs, don't fall for it. They are misinformed or not fully informed. The much-hyped harmful bacteria they speak of is not going to have any bearing or impact on the health of your dog or pet in general. Although this book is not claiming that vets are bad, we must recognize that a veterinary practice is a business. By definition, businesses exist to make money as a first priority to stay in business, and although we endeavor to think it's their mad love for our pets that drives their decisions, it's not always the case, as it should be, of course. It's our job to protect and educate ourselves so we can best utilize their knowledge and talents to make solid decisions for our pets' health, and our own health in a parallel manner with our human doctors.

Many vets are well-informed professionals. Other vets perhaps haven't taken the time to fully research the topics on which they advise. More than I care to admit, I have seen vets share information that they clearly have not invested time and research into understanding. They've given inaccurate, incomplete, or misleading information when they should have referred the client to an expert in that specific field. Traditional human doctors are guilty of the same thing. I have noticed much more of this in the veterinarian community for our beloved pets than with human doctors.

The harmful bacteria argument usually centers around producing one result—selling you something to produce more revenue. The bottom line is that when it comes to bacteria, it's somewhat of a miracle of nature. It is here to help and clean the body, not to destroy and kill or create other diseases for which dogs need antibiotics to stop those detoxing behaviors, as we are often told. The bacteria are present because there is waste present. The issue is the waste itself. It is not the bacteria, because the bacteria is designed to resolve and remove the waste, which is a necessary bodily process (ReAct Group, n.d.) (Wernimont et al., 2020).

Why a Traditional Vet May Not Be the Best Choice When Transitioning Your Pet to a Health- and Natural Immunity-Based Lifestyle versus a Sick-Based Lifestyle of Toxic Vaccination Schedules, Toxic Heartworm Treatment, and Toxic Chemical Flea and Tick Treatments

When you start the journey of course-correction with your dog's nutrition, it's important to know upfront that not everyone will be supportive. You may have to go it alone. It's best to be fully informed so you know you're making the best decisions for your pet. You're becoming your own advocate and your pet's informed advocate. That will take persistence, work, and strength. It's an achievement to take real control and responsibility rather than give that up to a human doctor or vet. Some people will be skeptical at best, while others will be judgmental at worst.

Sometimes, even holistic vets' frown on or even mock homemade dog food plans and nutrition. (I have found the majority to be quite supportive.) Lack of support or judgment from vets can especially show up when the nutrition plan includes implementing bones and raw meat. This happens because sometimes they aren't completely informed about how that properly works. Again, not every vet takes the time to learn the full process and outcomes of raw feeding. As you implement raw feeding, most likely, you'll be much more informed than vets. This will become more present as you continue to increase your knowledge and you experience firsthand the healing that raw feeding provides for your pet. During vet visits, some dog owners choose not to disclose information about their dog's diet to avoid hassle and frustration. Again, you're in charge now. What you disclose is your choice. Knowledge is truly power.

Why are Certain Veterinarians Adverse to a Species Appropriate Diet?

As you learn, it will build your confidence to advocate for yourself and your pet. This is truly necessary for optimal health and healing.

Keep in mind you're not going to find healthy dogs in a vet's office. This means the vets are not seeing and examining healthy dogs on a regular basis. Ask yourself, "What in an annual visit is really prevention?" Most times, you, unfortunately, find that nothing warranted such a title for those visits.

Heartworm medications, vaccinations, and flea and tick medications build toxicity in your pet's body. Thinking about that allows us to say, "Prevention? No. Disease creation and toxicity? Yes." A healthy dog with a healthy immune system and a clean terrain can handle all those items successfully. Think about it. How many wolves out there go to the vet for their "preventative health visits"? None. Yet, they do great. Our dogs live in a much easier world where they're loved, get exercise, and get fed properly (even more so after you implement a species appropriate diet).

It's only when we really sit down in the quiet space of our lives that we start connecting the dots and honestly thinking things through. We simply don't take what one educated person with credentials behind their name says. We need to ask ourselves, *"I heard what was said. Does it make sense?"*

If you read my biography, you know that I am one of those people who also has quite a few credentials. Just like in any job, career, or credentialed person, there are people who are brilliant and people who are average. When it comes to you and your pets, my stance is that you both deserve brilliant professionals! You and your pets deserve someone who loves what they do. The professionals who do the extra learning and go the extra mile are truly the ones who shine. They're exceptional people who we all need in our lives. Look for those people.

They're the difference makers. With the knowledge you're gaining here, it will be a huge win/win for both your health and your dog's health. Even with brilliant professionals, do your research. Ask hard questions. Truly explore and think things through. Ask yourself if what they're saying makes sense. That's the path to start making better, smarter, and more informed decisions for you and your dog.

Let's go back to the topic of vets mostly seeing sick dogs ... this means that they are not really getting firsthand information and evidence of what is working well to keep those dogs living a happy and healthy lifestyle. The vets are mostly seeing dogs that are sick. Quick quiz question: What do you think most of those dogs are eating? If you said that they are most likely eating commercialized dog feed, then you're correct! Most of the time, the vets recommend it. Once again, a vicious cycle is at play. It is important to know when something is going wrong with your dog. It's also critical to know if your dog needs to go to the vet or if you can handle it at home more comfortably and effectively. If you go to a vet, they usually instantly jump to the conclusion that it is one or more so-called culprits:

1. bacteria / germs,
2. genetics, or
3. raw diet (or a diet with which they have no direct firsthand experience or training).

When you have gone to the vet's office, it's because your dog was sick or acting "off." The vet probably mentioned one of those items as culprits. The truth? Most times they're not. We already learned that in a healthy pup, bacteria and germs are irrelevant. So are genetics.

Even if your pet has certain negative genes, they can stay turned off by a proper environment and by what you put in and on your pet. The diet is what creates health and healing. The truth is that when vets rattle off one or more of those three items, they are kind of using them as scapegoats. Remember, disease reversal and health and wellness are not areas vets are trained in. It's not up to them to be involved in such matters. Historically, just like medical doctors, vets are treating symptoms. They are not getting to the source and implementing an inside-out solution. It's not their job!

When your goal becomes to create a healthy and natural immunity-based lifestyle for your dog, know that you're not alone (even if the vets give you pushback). Those previously mentioned in the pet healing world, including myself, are available for consultations to assist you every step of the way. This book gives you all the guidance you will need to implement a healthy lifestyle for your pet.

Which Vets Might Support and Encourage Healing Diets? (Holistic, Homeopathy, and Chinese Medicine Veterinarians)

While traditional veterinarians will implement drugs and medical procedures for your dog, holistic vets, on the other hand, will usually implement supplements, nutritional diets, herbs, or a combination. Right off the bat, holistic vets sound like a better choice for healing and reversing disease states, right? Not always. Are herbs and supplements safer or less toxic? The answer is yes. Before I tell you why, let me share a nuance you need to know about.

"Safer" is an ambiguous word. Here's an example: Food A is commercialized pet feed. Now, there's Food A 2.0! It is labeled and marketed as safer. The problem is this: Even if it's 1% safer, it's still accurate to say it's safer. That's not exactly the point. The point is knowing how much safer it is. Plus, being safer will not restore health and wellness or reverse disease if you're trying to save your dog's life. Safer can be hard to measure and, at times, impossible to know. If you have two harmful drinks in front of you, one will more than likely be safer than the other. That does not change the fact they both are inherently harmful.

When a vet talks about safer options or treatments, it does not mean they are truly safe for your dog or that either option should be chosen. I know reading this book gives you a lot to memorize, think through, and let sink in. My advice is to read the book over again. The more you read it, the more you will connect all the dots. At which point, true learning will be committed to mind. The educator in me can share that to truly memorize things (I have told my students this over the years), it takes seven, plus or minus two, to truly remember something. This means you need to read it, write it, or say it seven, plus or minus two, times. This helps engage all the learning senses. That's what the average person requires to truly learn and commit something to memory. Don't feel you have to learn everything in one reading. That's the great thing about books. They are there for reference whenever you need them.

There are no supplements or herbs on the planet scientifically proven to cure or prevent any diseases, whether canine or human. Dietary supplements are not authorized to be promoted with the intention of healing, identifying, preventing, or remedying illnesses, unlike medications. Therefore, supplements should not assert to cure diseases, such as 'reduces high cholesterol' or 'treats heart disease.' Such claims are not valid for dietary supplements (U.S. Food and Drug Administration, 2017) (Freeman, 2017). Is it possible some of your dog's troublesome symptoms will diminish or lessen with herbs and supplements? Sure, it's possible. Still, there's a strong case you're still putting toxins into your dog's system. Shifting your dog's body to attend to the greater toxin to eliminate it from the body is what will help the symptoms improve or go away. A body will attend to the greater risk to preserve life—that's often what happens with drugs. A few weeks or months later, the same issue starts up again, likely something you have given antibiotics for in the past, or something new is reoccurring. This can be dangerous. Whether products are 10% harmful or 100% harmful, they are both harmful.

Are there vets who are both traditional and holistic? Yes. Interestingly enough, a hybrid vet oftentimes does not ensure creating the best results or lifestyle for your dog. Many times, it's a marketing technique to get new and "more conscious" pet owners in the door. Of course, there are traditional vets who switch to holistic practices and want to improve the health of dogs and have the best intentions also. There is no Raw Feeding for Dogs University. No person on the planet has a degree from there because it does not exist. In any case, if it isn't clear to you yet, you, my friend, have as much capacity as they do to learn about the absolute best practices for feeding your dog, which is what this book is all about. Vets have no special section in libraries or the internet where only they can access "secrets" and insights. It's all available to you, right now. Just make sure to choose legitimate research and review the top information out there. Is your dog worth it? We know so!

When you research local vets and they have terms in their titles or clinic names like complementary, integrative, or something similar, it's still your responsibility to do your research. The training and research show, once again, that most of the time they are still only treating symptoms and not the root cause of the disease, yet addressing the root cause is the only way it can be reversed or put into remission. Think functional medicine for pets because that's what it does for humans.

Traditional vets are not exploring and working at discovering the underlying causes of your dog's health issues. It's not their job, just as it isn't the job of a traditional MD in the human world. And if they're not doing that, what's the point of spending your time and money? Overall, I do not recommend them for overcoming disease states or reversing disease because it's not their job.

The presence of ailments and disease means the body is working hard to remedy, compensate for, and overcome something which is hurting or diminishing its overall physical health or capacity for healing. "Disease is any harmful deviation from the normal structural or functional state of an organism, generally associated with certain signs and symptoms and differs in nature from physical injury" (Burrows, Professor of Microbiology, University of Chicago, n.d.). A key point is that disease and physical injuries or traumas are two very different things. The best nutrition plan on the planet is not going to fix a dog's broken leg.

A vet may be able to block a disease or symptoms with medication, which is sometimes necessary in life-and-death situations. It's important to understand that this does not reverse the disease state, and in most cases only creates more toxicity. If you're looking to restore health and reverse disease states, a functionally trained vet whose focus is closer to this book's philosophy and methods is a rare and precious find! When you get the feeling your vets only want to see you pull out your cash or card, that's when you need to go elsewhere. When you sense the vet or a pet health coach is willing to do the work to get to the source of your dog's health issues, that's when you've found a wonderful ally and champion.

Always keep in mind, whether it is for your body or for your dog's body, the goal is to get to the root of the disease to reverse it and restore health. After all, we both only get one life! What's the source? What is causing the symptoms? As you now know, most of the time, the source of the diseases or health issues centers around what you and your dog are eating, digesting, and absorbing

Do Pet Nutritionists Get It Exactly Right?

While pet and dog-specific nutritionists (called canine nutritionists) may be considered safer, there's more to the story. A pet nutritionist obviously sounds safer than a traditional vet, but is that true? Pet nutritionists usually are so engrossed and enrolled in theories they have learned, and they are creating them, that they fail to see the larger picture concerning the dog's overall health. There's more happening than what they see under a microscope. From what I've seen, many times they make home feeding much more complicated and nuanced than it needs to be. Their intentions are good, and one can only do as they learn, but it has been said that great leaders and educators are great simplifiers. When it comes to pet nutritionists, they usually will not necessarily simplify. Let's face the facts. If a nutrition plan is too complicated, it's either not going to get implemented properly or consistently or we'll get it started only to quickly replace it by convenience feeding. Another issue is that they may suggest nutrition plans that feature feeding your dog incompatible foods at the same time, like mixing meats with plants or adding in supplements or not removing animal fat.

I understand at this point you may feel very alone. You may be thinking, *If the people who are supposed to be the professionals and be highly trained cannot be trusted, then who can I trust or who has gotten it right?* The answer is to trust science and nature and those who advocate their principles.

No vets of any sort or pet nutritionists are trained to go after the source of diseases or ailments your dog is experiencing. Pet health coaching has started going in the right direction, using a more holistic or functional medicine approach. The industry isn't quite there yet. From my experience, the programs that were great seemed to have dissolved.

The answer is in the diet! The health and future of your dog all comes down to what you're feeding him or putting on him and what the body digests and absorbs. The same goes for you! These are core principles out of the human functional medicine world. Did you know most products and medications proven for humans come from animals or, sadly, from animal testing? This is because what often works for animals first will work for humans too. Therefore I choose to show similarities between animals and humans ... because it's so relevant. An amazing situation, too, is that as pet owners work on improving the lives of their dogs, many also eventually transition themselves to a healthier lifestyle.

The diet you'll learn more about soon for your dog can help you remove symptoms by strategically removing the source of the problem. In other words, the diet gets to the root cause of your dog's disease and can reverse it or put the disease state in remission. The same can also be done for humans and their autoimmune diseases. Let's learn more about other bits of information that aren't necessarily true about a dog's dietary needs.

Are Age-Specific Diets Necessary?

You've probably heard of age-specific dog diets. Is it fact or fiction? Ultimately, it's fiction. Throughout the lifespan of a dog, they will generally eat the same foods over and over.

When you hear about age-specific diets, it is largely a marketing ploy designed by the pet feed industry. Consider how this plays out. A dog owner feeds her dog commercialized dog feed for years. As a dog ages, the dog owner knows her pet's health is diminishing. She looks for solutions and hears about age-specific pet feed. She begins buying it and feeding it to her dog. However, here is the interesting thing that happens. The commercialized dog feed is what diminished the dog's health over time in the first place.

So now, the health issues that the pet feed industry created are trying to be "remedied" by the exact same industry that caused them! It's an unhealthy cyclical spiral of events focused on profit. It's not about the health of your dog. The age-specific food focuses on helping your dog's body with its weakened ability to stay active and eliminate wastes and toxins the industry initially created.

Are there exceptions? Yes. When it comes to puppies, they need to be weaned on regurgitated food; that's how it's done in the wild. In our everyday environments, it's not possible (at least nowadays) to replicate and mimic regurgitated foods.

Even with following these recommendations, it may be essential to switch up or modify an aging dog's nutrition plan. This may include any of the following: removal of excess fats, only feeding with clean animals, forgoing grinding up meat, lowering food intake levels, adding plant-only feeding days, fasting, or some other type of modification. The important aspect is that the change is based on nature, science, and your dog's life history and current disease states (if they have any). It could be your dog is healthy and you simply want to detox her before they are labeled with a specific disease pattern. I can tell you from my experience, the ideal way is to bring up pups correctly, without potential disease states settling in. If you're just finding out about this now and your dog is sick, rest assured there is still plenty of hope! There's not only hope to reverse disease states, but also hope to expand their lifetimes.

Are Dogs Carnivores or Are They Really Omnivores?

If you remember a science class from high school or college, you probably remember learning that mammals can be classified by what they eat. Here's a quick refresher:

1. Carnivore (meat eater)
2. Omnivore (meat and plant eater, or all eater)
3. Frugivore (fruit eater)
4. Herbivore (plant eater)
5. Folivore (leaf eater)

Let's focus on carnivores and omnivores now. Carnivores rely solely on animal tissue or meat for their food and energy requirements. Tigers and lions are examples.

Omnivores, on the other hand, can eat both meat and plants. Omnivores include bears, chickens, and rats. They have an adaptive digestive system that can break down both plant and animal material. Their diets usually consist of a variety of components such as fruits, vegetables, grains, and proteins. Omnivores usually consume a wide variety of food sources, which allows them to survive in a wide range of habitats. They are also able to take advantage of seasonal food sources, which help them to survive during times of food scarcity.

Carnivores and omnivores branch down into two different types:

1. Facultative
2. Obligate

Facultative means optional. In biology, it means "capable of living under varying conditions" (Collins Dictionary, n.d.). Facultative carnivores are animals that are capable of surviving on a diet that includes both animal and plant-based foods. However, they generally prefer to consume meat when it is available. Wolves and dogs are in the Canis classification. This makes them facultative carnivores because although they can eat both plants and meat, they prefer a diet of meat and will actively seek it out when it is available. Essentially, they're facultative carnivores with omnivorous tendencies.

Obligate means not optional. "As an adjective, obligate means 'by necessity'"(Educalingo, n.d.)

Another definition is "able to exist under only one set of environmental conditions" (Collins Dictionary, n.d.).

Obligate carnivores, also called hypercarnivores, are animals that must consume a diet that is exclusively composed of animal-based foods to survive. It is well-established that the felines, which encompass lions, tigers, and cats, fall into the category of obligate carnivores (Bradford, 2018). Cats are in the same taxonomy as most wild cats, called Felis. This means they all share the same traits, ancestry, and physiological makeup. They are all part of the Felid family, which are obligate carnivores. They are obligate carnivores because they lack the ability to produce certain nutrients, such as taurine and vitamin A, that are essential for their health and are only synthesized from animal sources, such as hearts (Legrand-Defretin, V., 1994).

Similarly, facultative and obligate omnivores are animals that consume both plant- and animal-based foods, but differ in their degree of reliance on either. Facultative omnivores, like humans, can survive on a diet that includes both plant and animal-based foods, but have a preference for one or the other. Obligate omnivores, like pigs and raccoons, require a diet that includes both plant and animal-based foods to survive and cannot thrive on a diet that is exclusively composed of one or the other.

To summarize, the main difference between facultative and obligate carnivores and omnivores is their level of reliance on a particular type of food. Facultative animals can survive on a mixed diet. Obligate animals require a specific type of food to maintain their health and survival.

So, are dogs carnivores or omnivores? This is where it gets tricky because it depends on who you ask! Even the scientific community argues about this and it's a discussion that is far from over. However, we do know that science places dogs in the class called Mammalia (mammals), and the order Carnivora (carnivore) (Myers, et al., 2023). We also know that dogs are further classified as facultative carnivores (Domínguez-Oliva, et al., 2023).

Cats and dogs both have pointy teeth, which indicate that both should eat meat. However, cats have a shorter snout which means they have the ability to crush their food, like bones and twigs. Dogs have a longer snout, meaning they have less crushability than cats. This indicates they would not eat meat 100% of the time.

It may be surprising to find out that one quarter of wild cats had plant matter in their feces, that was not from vegetation such as fruits and berries. This included twigs and grass, which cats are able to consume as part of meeting their non-nutritional needs (Bonnaud, et al., 2007).

Let's look at research on wolves again. Bosch notes that the domestication of dogs occurred roughly 13,000 to 17,000 years ago, when they began to gravitate toward communities where people lived. Nowadays, modern canines exhibit a range of both digestive and metabolic characteristics that are more akin to omnivores like humans and pigs. This has also led to dogs being classified as omnivores in the scientific community (Bosch et al., 2014). If a dog is consuming grass, it doesn't necessarily mean that their diet lacks essential nutrients. It's possible that the behavior is simply instinctual. This action reflects the dog's genetic heritage as omnivores and is an inherent trait passed down through generations of dogs, going back to wolves (Meyers, 2022). Based on my research, it's my belief that the main motivation for eating grass is instinct.

To paraphrase Coates, while it is widely known that dogs are classified under the order Carnivora, it is important to note that they are omnivorous. This is due to their unique ability to convert specific amino acids, the fundamental components of protein, thereby allowing dogs to meet their amino acid requirements without consuming meat (Coates, 2013).

Ultimately, based on the research above, it appears canines are facultative carnivores with omnivorous tendencies. Knowing that and practicing a true species appropriate diet that's about 4% to 8% carbs; 20% plant-matter based; fasting from meat days to plant days; and following a diet that's 80% muscle meat, 10% bone, and 10% internal organs on meat days is what saved my dog's life.

Some of the Most Popular Raw Feeding Models for Canines

What is raw feeding? What is important for dog owners to know? Let me show you the lay of the land concerning raw feeding. If you've checked out online groups and websites, you probably already know there are two well-known methods and a few lesser known philosophies when it comes to raw feeding. Although these are healthier and more advantageous than any commercialized pet feed, none are entirely ideal to stave off disease states or correct them.

Four Raw Feeding Models:

1. Prey Model Raw: PMR
2. Biologically Appropriate Raw Food (also called Bones And Raw Food, and Basic Ancestral Raw Food): BARF
3. Mixed Ingredient (cooked or raw)
4. Biologically Conflicting (sometimes a combination of cooked and raw)

There are other raw nutrition plans out there besides these four. I considered adding other models, but there is less research available on them. Additionally, other models have not been around as long or as well-defined as PMR, BARF, mixed ingredient and biologically conflicting. If I find new models in the future, I'll work at adding them to the updated version of this book.

Characteristics:

- PMR: Their stance is that dogs are carnivores, pure and simple. The PMR model consists of feeding your dog raw meat, bones, and organs. No plants, fruits or veggies are allowed. PMR's stance is to feed whole prey. This includes the entire animal as well as feathers and fur. The idea is that there is zero waste. This is for owners who enjoy zero waste. They may enjoy hunting and/or feeding exotic prey.
- BARF: Their stance is that dogs are omnivores. The BARF model consists of feeding your dog raw meat, bones, and

organs, as well as fruits and veggies. It does not recommend using whole prey, and thus, no fur or feathers. BARF is raw food that may be frozen and dehydrated. That's how you can easily recognize them in a store. Many of these owners are short on time or do not prioritize a true species appropriate diet, but still know that commercialized pet feed is an unhealthy choice.

- Mixed Ingredient: Like BARF, their stance is that dogs are omnivores. Homemade raw is not as defined or as strict as BARF and PMR. Meaning, homemade raw can be somewhat different from one dog owner to the next. In fact, both BARF and PMR can possibly be categorized as homemade raw. This nutrition plan usually includes raw meat, bones, vegetables and fruits. Sometimes, they're mixed together elaborately and look like a gourmet meal, or separately all laid out like a charcuterie board. I tend to see these dog owners very invested in the quality and presentation of their dog's food.

- Biologically Conflicting: This model is just how it sounds. Some food items align with a dog's biology and some are conflicting. Many times, they rotate through certain foods. For example, Mondays may be chicken days, Tuesdays may be fruit days, and so on. Sometimes, biologically conflicting feeders include a fast day for their dogs, and sometimes they do not. They do tend to feed a lot of sweet potato mixtures and often offer less meat days than plant days. These diets can advocate for removing all fat and all skin, as well as feeding vegetables that are not in a raw state. And oftentimes, too many carbohydrates and items containing cellulose are fed.

Similarities:

- All models emphasize foods that are natural and avoid commercialized pet feed.
- None of the nutrition plans advocate for feeding dogs live prey.
- All avoid artificial additives and preservatives.

Within these different raw models, which is the best for your dog? That's not exactly the best question. The truth is this—each has varying degrees of being right and wrong. Does that sound confusing, or what? Keep reading, as I share all the details.

Let's consider wolves for a moment. Long before domesticated dogs had the experiences of commercialized kibbled dog feed, attitude outfits, and comfy doggie beds, their ancestral counterparts were living in the wild. Research on wolves provides a captivating insight into the physiological characteristics of domesticated dogs. We know dogs prefer meat. We also know they can live for long periods of time only eating plants, just like wolves.

In one feeding, a wolf can consume up to a whooping 19% of its own body weight (Mech, 2007, p. 201). Many sources say wolves can devour up to 20 pounds of flesh in one feeding (Scully, 2017) (The National Wildlife Federation, n.d.).

On average, wolves consume approximately 10 pounds of meat per day, although their feeding habits are characterized by a feast-or-famine lifestyle. It is not uncommon for wolves to go without food for several days, and then consume more than 20 pounds thanks to a fresh kill (International Wolf Center).

Taxonomy classifications are a wide, detailed, and nuanced field of study, and within each category exists varied ranges of species. Inside of the classification of carnivores, some species live entirely on prey animals. However, other classifications hold that some species will eat meat as a primary source. In fact, there's lots of research and evidence that shows wolves, and their pups, eat plants.

The consumption of blueberries by gray wolves is commonly acknowledged. In fact, new research shows they sometimes vomit the blueberries to give nourishment to their pups (Buehler, 2020).

For a while, scholars have been cognizant of wolves' tendency to consume wild blueberries and other fruits as an addition to their predominant meat-based intake. Current reports by Gable and colleagues indicate that blueberries can account for up to 83% of the July sustenance of the eight wolf packs under their scrutiny found roaming in and around Voyageurs National Park (Kraker, 2020).

In fact, red wolves exhibit a varied diet that includes smaller prey like insects, rodents, and rabbits. Interestingly, these carnivores have also been observed consuming berries occasionally, which demonstrates flexibility in their feeding habits (Bradford, 2017).

During the summer months, the analysis of wolf droppings reveals a diet consisting of 8% grasses and berries, and in some cases, as much as 20% plant material. Moreover, Stadler et al. discovered that 74% of wolf feces collected in the summer contained plant matter (Stahler, et al., 2006).

All models will most likely create health issues at some point.

1. PMR feeders overwhelm their dogs' systems. Their digestive systems are inundated nonstop with foods that are unbalanced and filled with excess fat. Owners generally do not remove the excess fat before giving it to their pets because the food is often given as an entire animal (fur and all). Their bodies never have a moment for a reprieve or a detox. If you want to get technical, you're feeding your dog like a cat, an obligate carnivore. It

also does not mimic a species appropriate diet because there is not any fasting. We've learned from a previous chapter that 20% of a species appropriate diet is plant-based. We've also learned that in looking at dental makeup, a dog has a longer snout which has less crushing ability, which means they aren't eating meat with every meal.

2. BARF feeders feed their dogs a wide (and sometimes wild) variety of foods and are more likely to feed their dogs like they feed themselves. This includes but isn't limited to oils, supplements, herbs, processed items meant for good health, and food-based products. Many times, this includes foods which are unassimilable and should never even be given to dogs. (B.A.R.F. Basic Ancestral Raw Food, n.d.). Dogs owners are often concerned about the lack of nutrients that their dogs are getting and if they're truly getting a balanced diet. They often have dogs that are inflamed in some way. They end up looking for solutions in non-food products. I often see clients overloving their pets through supplements, when in reality, the supplements are causing toxicity in their systems because these items are not assimilable. This simply does not work. It does not create optimal health for one's dog to supplement or feed items that are unassimilable. What it does do is create toxicity and overburdens the digestive system, as well as creates inflammatory disease states. Indigestible products, like oil, are commonly used incorrectly or are not combined correctly. BARF feeders also run the risk of mixing plants with meat in their dogs' stomachs, which creates toxicity due to waste and indigestion. This can also create bloating and gas. Pets can also suffer from vitamin D deficiency if they don't consume enough skin (which some BARF feeders use and some don't),

and may lack manganese if they don't consume indigestible parts such as hair.

3. Mixed ingredient feeders' dogs can experience problems as well. When the food is not prepared well or monitored correctly, the dogs can suffer from nutritional imbalances. If the dog owner does not formulate the recipes accurately, the diet won't support optimal health. Nutritional imbalances can lead to issues like weakened bones and immune system dysfunction. They may also feed their dogs cooked vegetables, which is not recommended for a species appropriate diet. Even worse, at times, are all of the ingredients being mixed in the dog's stomach, which we have learned dogs have a one-chambered stomach. Mixing all of the ingredients can lead to toxicity as well as bloating and gas.

4. Biologically conflicting feeders most likely will run into problems when they do not follow their calendar and/or mix up days, which can create digestive issues. Also, if they do not have time to prepare in advance, meals can be compromised. They sometimes do not follow the directions and will leave excessive skin and fat on the animals they're preparing. Food preparation can be time-consuming, which varies based on the skillset of the preparer, as with any meal prep. Often, lots of sweet potatoes and/or other carbs are fed, as well as other cooked vegetables. This can easily exceed the 4% to 8% recommendation, relative to carbs, which we see in the wolf population. Also, their diets can also make up more than 20% of plants, which is not recommended based on the data about wolves. They may also cook veggies, which is not recommended for a species appropriate diet. The amount of veggies should be incredibly limited. Some of them stick to a strict plan for the sake of

sticking to a plan, rather than being flexible on food choices and/or adjusting when their pets need more food. These plans tend to be more focused on the owner dictating and sticking to a schedule, rather than partnering with the natural choices and natural balance of their pets.

Regardless of the model being implemented, the end result is usually the same—an unhealthy amount of waste in their dogs' systems or some level of unnecessary toxicity! These models can overwhelm and overburden a dog's system as well as cause sickness and disease. As you already know, waste and toxins are the enemies. Sadly, those dogs still struggle from many allergenic symptoms, food sensitivities, and yeast issues, despite the diets above. This adds further proof that none of these models have it completely correct.

My stance is that there are no one-size-fits-all or perfect nutrition models for dogs. Not even mine! Why? Because our dogs are domesticated and because your dog's life is in your hands. They can no longer eat the species appropriate diet because they are not out hunting as nature intended and eating off the land. We are feeding them what we choose to feed them. At the same time, it's an incredible privilege and a large responsibility. Only you can observe your pet. Only you can apply your common sense. When you observe your dog each day, you know what's normal. I cannot tell you what to feed your dog. I can tell you that one or more deficiencies can be created by only feeding meat, mixing plants with meat, feeding too many carbohydrates, feeding too much plant matter, feeding unassimilable items like synthetic supplements and refined oils, not feeding grasses and fruits, not feeding raw foods, and/or not feeding some skin and fur. Knowing this gives you a huge advantage in guiding your pet's vitality and longevity.

What Do We Know About the History of Dogs and Their Real Nutritional Needs?

These non-refutable historical facts include the following:

- Dogs did not eat supplements in the wild.
- Dogs didn't eat oils in the wild.
- Dogs have eaten and can eat plants.
- Dogs are no strangers to starvation eating. They can live for long time frames between killing and eating their prey.
- Dogs historically ate much leaner than they do nowadays with commercialized foods readily available.
- Eating on a consistent basis like they do now is a newer development in their long history.
- Eating one type of food in one sitting has been the pattern; they weren't about mixing food categories. Example: If the dog caught a squirrel, it counts as one type of food or one category of food.
- Prey (meat) has been the first choice for dogs to eat.
- Dogs hunt when they are honestly hungry. Their bodies are calling out for nutrients and matter, and thus they are prompted to hunt only at that point.
- Dogs are selective eaters historically who only eat what entices them. Those foods were natural, animal, and in and of nature.
- Dogs ate uncooked bones.

- The alpha dogs got the best nutrition first and ate the internal organs, as they are the most nutritious. Then the beta dogs got their share.
- Dogs in the wild get lots of exercise hunting for prey.
- Dogs didn't eat fatty animals or eat the fat of animals in the wild because wild animals aren't fed commercialized grains, and they don't sit around gaining weight.

Along with those facts, it's relevant to know that a dog is a monogastric organism. This means it has a simple single-chambered stomach. Humans, rats, dogs, and pigs are among the monogastric omnivores. However, unlike ruminants, they are not able to digest cellulose as well (Wikipedia, n.d.). A ruminant is a plant-eating mammal with a hoofed foot structure and a stomach consisting of three or four chambers (Merriam-Webster, n.d.). These include cattle, giraffes, sheep, goats, etc. However, the ability of monogastric omnivores to digest cellulose varies among species.

As a dog owner, you must be careful when feeding vegetables with high cellulose content. These include but are not limited to celery, broccoli, cauliflower, peas, and asparagus. I learned this lesson the hard way when I used to cook vegetables and gave my dog too many peas and carrots in one day. He became bloated and constipated. His demeanor changed and it was obvious that he was struggling. It totally freaked me out. Legumes have the same effect on my dog, even though they have less cellulose than peas. To optimize your dog's health, I recommend serving vegetables with high cellulose in limited quantities or not including them in your dog's nutrition plan. If you decide to use them, mash them up with a potato masher. I would never feed a full plate of peas in one day, especially to a smaller dog. Additionally, it is important to observe your dog after they have eaten these vegetables in order to watch for any adverse reactions. A species appropriate diet calls for either not serving veggies that have high cellulose, or only serving small limited quantities of raw veggies.

All Human Grade Raw Diets Are Better than Over-Commercialized Pet Feeds. However, Some Actually Cause Disease Similar to Commercialized Pet Feeds

You may be thinking, *If I feed my dog raw food, my pooch will live an exceptionally healthy and long life.* That is not always the case. You need to know some key information.

When feeding your dog raw food, mistakes can happen. What is scary is that those mistakes can possibly cause disease in the long term, or they can block healing.

BARF and PMR feeders oftentimes assume when their dogs are exhibiting symptoms or are dealing with uncharacteristic behavior, the issues relate back to previous or recent vaccinations, genetics, or a deficiency in nutrients. It's easy for each type of feeder to think that they're doing everything humanly possible to optimize their pets' health … when really, they're not.

When your dog is exhibiting symptoms or you know something is off, first you want to check the most likely source—what she is eating. Be careful not to jump to conclusions and assume her diet is perfect and it must be something else. For the most part, your dog's diet holds the key to his longevity, vitality, and lifespan. Most actual causes of disease originate from your dog's food or nutrition.

Of course, vaccinations and breeding usually do create some type of health issues for dogs, as well as chemicals and toxins in their environment. Those do play a factor. However, you do not want to operate on assumptions. For answers and solutions, look to science and nature, along with the inside-out approach we have been talking about (which you'll learn more about later). Plus, be ready and willing to test these theories. Test to see what works best for your specific dog and to observe. Observation is the best technique to use to notice patterns and common behaviors, which will help you rule things out and come to the most accurate interpretation. This will require time but probably not as much as you think.

When a health issue comes to light with your dog, ask yourself this question: What's the most likely cause of this issue? Many causes can be eliminated or diminished without harmful or toxic pseudo-solutions (i.e., drugs or supplements).

This means you have the power! You can help control your dog's future to the best of your abilities and insights. Pretty amazing, right? I know it's both scary and amazing that you now know the key to your dog's health is his food and nutrition.

CHAPTER 5

Transitioning Your Dog's One-Chambered Stomach

YOU'VE GOTTEN THIS FAR IN THE BOOK. Congrats! At this point, you're probably wondering if you are ready to make the transition from what you're feeding your dog to a species appropriate diet. My answer is this—You are ready!

The first insight to know is about what your dog may experience during this change if it's not done correctly. Earlier, you learned how different foods get processed at different speeds inside of your dog's digestive system. When moving to a raw, natural diet, keep that in mind. Different foods can create problems inside of the digestive tract if they "meet" there, due to your dog's single-chamber stomach.

Remember, we do not want veggies to touch meat in the stomach. We don't want fruits to touch meat in the stomach, and so on. When that happens, it creates toxicity.

Ultimately, you want to aim for there to be no food particles, fragments, or remains from your dog's former diet in her digestive tract prior to feeding her raw meat. If those old particles or remnants are present, they will slow down and hinder the digestion of the newly introduced raw food. If the previous diet and new diet meet in your dog's stomach, it's not the end of the world, but it is bad news. Why? Putrefaction will start. As you already know, dogs' stomachs can handle that much better than humans. However, the dog's bodily response is to work hard to eliminate its presence. There are two ways this happens, and neither is pretty. It comes out either as vomit or diarrhea. (So much for a relaxing evening walk, but it's normal in this situation!)

Therefore, you want a clean break and a fresh new slate to transition into. There's no progression here; there's no mixing the old and new diets. One chapter ends. A new one begins. It must be cleared out. Like a colonoscopy!

As you can imagine, the vomiting and diarrhea cause many dog owners who tried raw natural feeding to have a bad experience. They think it was not the right fit for their dog, or they blame it on something else. The truth is they simply did not follow the correct steps to create a successful transition to the new diet … but you can, and will, as we are guiding you in that direction—and if you need more help, I am available for consults.

The diet model I followed to heal my dog is simply called Species Appropriate Feeding, based on what research says about wolves in the wild and their biology, and how that relates to meat amounts, plant amounts, and fruit amounts. Species appropriate means fresh meat without any added carbohydrates, synthetic supplementation, or unassimilable nutrients. The goal is that the feeding closely matches how dogs eat in the wild. I break that all down for you so you can choose how to feed your dog in a correct species appropriate diet. How do you transition from what you're doing now? In my research and experience, I believe this is the most healing nutrition plan that exists for dogs. Here's the breakdown:

TIP 2

On the final day of a regular diet, here are suggested steps to transition to species appropriate feeding:

- Step 1: One full day (24 hours) of fasting.

- Step 2: Here are two options:
  a. Option 1: Offer only fresh filtered water for that day (and every day), and make sure the dog doesn't run out.
  b. Option 2: Offer only vegetables and fruits for a full day of feeding (if you are already giving certain veggies or fruits, start there. If not, I originally gave a mixture of sweet potatoes and peas and carrots, and I mashed the peas for better digestion and eventually added de-saponified quinoa. I found this to create a lot of gas in my dog and specifically, the sweet potatoes were very heavy for him. They often made him sick or weirdly constantly hungry. I stopped using sweet potatoes). Do note that when you're making quinoa, you can steam or boil it. If you want to stay raw, you can use flaked quinoa.

You're now on the last step; you have completed Day 1 of raw natural feeding, whether you fed once or twice a day. A fast of clean filtered water is a highly effective way to give your dog's body (or yours) a break. It gives the digestive tract and stomach some downtime to heal, rest, and make time for other foods to clear out.

Implementing a full day of only fruits and vegetables helps to clean out your dog's system too. Interestingly enough, this makes his first raw meal that much more alluring and enticing.

You've done a great job getting to this point in the book. Keep in mind that as you are transitioning, keep it positive for you and your dog. Yes, it can be hard to start something new. Yes, you're both learning together. Give yourself and your dog grace during the transition. Expect growing pains. Expect having to start and stop. Expect only having a little progress one week and a lot of progress the next week. This is all normal and part of learning new habits. As long as you keep moving forward, even if you start and stop or take one step backwards to move forward, you will reach your goals by implementing consistency, planning and observation. Sticking to rigid schedules, trying to force things in any direction, and/or getting frustrated or emotional before engaging your thought process to diagnose what went wrong first, only ends in failure. Always think before you react. Your dog constantly observes and reacts to your emotions. The more frustrated and negative you are, the more your dog will be. That won't help you reach your goals. Stay calm, positive and focused. Celebrate even the small steps forward for you and your dog!

Bile Vomiting Happens for Some Dogs Who Are Transitioned: Is It Anything to Be Concerned About?

You may have heard about dogs vomiting bile, or even have seen it happen. It happens! Typically, it looks like a little yellow foam. It's exceptionally common, even among dog owners who are PMR feeders, and it can sometimes happen during the healing process. It sometimes happens because your dog is so excited for his real food and he smells it and it gets his gastric juices flowing—it's just too much for him to keep down without food. My dog eventually got extra sharp about handling it and would go get sips of water, and it stopped. Dogs, just like people, handle everything differently. Those who don't mind puking go ahead and puke; my guy, on the other hand, got super nervous about puking, so he handled it a better way. As he healed, it rarely happened. I will address this in greater detail. Here's what you need to know about this topic.

Your dog's last day on his regular diet signifies the end of how your dog has been eating as he knows it. You must realize it's more than likely you have been feeding your dog way too much fat. It's likely the case whether you've been feeding your dog commercialized food (the amount of fat is literally posted on every bag, can, or the like) or food made at home (likely you didn't know how important it is to remove it). In fact, most pet owners feed their dogs more fat than their dogs' bodies are designed to handle. The more immediate side effect of this is that a dog's body creates too much bile as toxins from animal fat are now circulating through your dog. Whether human or pet, toxins in our bodies are stored in adipose tissue (fat) to keep toxins away from our organs like we talked about earlier. You are likely now able to start piecing together much of your valuable dog health and wellness knowledge and know much more than some pet professionals know about pet nutrition. You are now becoming a truly competent and informed pet owner, relying on your own empowered judgment. You can feel much more confident about your future choices and be able to ask better questions when you do need a vet visit or extra help for rehabilitation or injury, if it should occur to your beloved pet. So, well done, you!

Let's look at nature for a greater explanation. When a wolf or wild dog is seeking his prey, that expectation of feeding means everything. It triggers digestive responses in his body. These include the release of bile acids. Our domestic dogs have triggers too. You haven't seen your dog for over an hour. You open a bag of chips and what happens? She is instantly by your side! She thinks you're opening her treat bag. For dogs nowadays, the triggers include sounds, smelling food, and even seeing you start the feeding ritual. This could include any aspect of the feeding ritual, whether it's opening your squeaky pantry door or something else.

Here's the issue. Let's say a trigger happens, but it's a false alarm. You needed something from the pantry, and the door squeaked like usual. Now your dog is wagging her tail beside you, anxious and looking forward to being fed. You know it's a false alarm. Your dog and its body do not.

What happens? Its body, in anticipation of food, begins releasing the bile. You see, the bile's responsibility is to break down fats. Now bile is in the stomach, waiting for food to arrive … and nothing happens. At this point, the bile most likely is in contact with the dog's stomach lining. This contact can cause irritation or discomfort because the bile is concentrated. The food your dog was mistakenly expecting had the power to dilute the bile, but it's not present. The body now needs to protect itself from the bile. How does it do that? Bingo! The dog vomits out the bile.

Not all dogs vomit bile like this. Different dogs have different body types and chemistries. There's no one-size-fits-all considering the frequency. Granted, the more you observe your dog, the more you'll learn and be able to recognize her patterns.

Some vets or experts may recommend feeding your dog with greater frequency to prevent the bile vomiting. This creates a scenario where your dog almost always has food in his or her stomach. However, it's not getting to the root cause of the situation being created. Training them to have a little extra water as I mentioned worked for my little guy. As you adapt this diet to your dog and your unique situation, you will learn many little solutions simply by observing your furry pal.

If you read about and research in your favorite search engine online, you'll see several comments where dog owners say their dogs threw up bile on a regular basis ... until they chose to diminish how much fat their dogs were eating. This stabilization period can take a few weeks to a few months. However, eventually, the bile vomiting will come to an end once and for all.

What about fasting? Let's say you put your dog on a one-day fast. If he throws up bile during the fast, it is possible you may not be able to fast her at the start. The dog's body has its own wisdom. As your dog's digestive system starts recovering and optimizing, implementing fasting days will become easier and more user-friendly for your dog. Dogs experience countless benefits when they do a full water-only fast. In light of that, I do recommend attempting to implement the fast again. As you continue to improve your dog's nutrition, you will see bile vomiting come to an end. Doesn't that sound like relief for both of you? Yes, it does, and with time, patience, and weekly improved healing, you will be able to visually see your dog healing and improving. In my case, my boy looked at me on his first raw meat day like *What, that's for me?* and then like *Mom, you finally got it right!* So, if you observe and learn your dog's behaviors as they heal and enjoy their new way of eating, you'll see behaviors and visual improvements that will solidify that you're on the right path!

CHAPTER 6

Learning About a Species Appropriate Diet and How It Works

I'M SURE YOU'VE HEARD OF CROP ROTATION BEFORE. It's a technique where farmers grow a series of different crop types in the same area. They implement a sequence of growing seasons too. This method creates several benefits like reducing reliance on one set of nutrients from the soil, lowering pest and weed pressure, and lowering the probability of developing resistant pests and weeds. The rotation helps the farmers maximize what they have and create optimal results.

When it comes to a species appropriate diet, it is inherently rotational. Why? Because of the feast-and-famine that wolves experience. If their first choice in prey is not available, they look for the next prey down the line. They may be different types of meats, fruits or plants. That in itself is rotation within each category. It naturally happens. This is why I share diet examples and tell you to rotate food categories later in chapter 8. It's inherently species appropriate.

What makes species appropriate feeding brilliant and canine-friendly is that it acknowledges and honors the fact that dogs have a one-chamber stomach, which is naturally inherent in the wild because once a dog makes a kill and fills up, they don't need anything else until they're hungry again. They're not out there making gourmet meals of mixed food categories, nor do they have anyone doing it for them. Rotating categories is something that naturally happens in a species appropriate diet and I'm taking time to explain this to you today. Recall that, by design, a dog's stomach is engineered in a way to only digest one type of food at a time, hence the biological name monogastric. To be clear, it's not one food at a time with one after the other. We don't want different food types to touch. We want it to mimic the natural species appropriate diet found in the wild. The focus is on one category of food at a time.

Let's consider the history of wolves and wild dogs again, where we can see this in action in greater depth. Mixing different food types out in nature was rarely an option. A wild dog's food time usually came down to him hunting, killing, and eating a small animal. He would eat the entire carcass. Internal organs first, of course, as they were the most nutritious. Furthermore, the animal would have been an herbivore (plant-eater). In this context, the dead animal's edible sections are to be viewed as a single kind of food. A squirrel would have been a single type of food; for example, meat. For wolf pack eaters, killing as a pack means larger prey, so they would eat a portion of a large kill, such as a deer or buffalo. With this view, it's easy to see that their meals did not include a mix of carbs and proteins (meats) together. They obviously did not include things not found in nature, either, like oils or supplements. It is also safe to say they did not stop to microwave or cook their food, or give themselves flea treatments or heartworm medicines. They seem to do just fine and there's a reason for that! These are the roots of where our dogs evolved from, and some dogs are far closer to a wolf's genetics than others. After all, our dogs today are .002% genetically different from wolves, and that includes their digestive system. To say it inversely, wolves and dogs share 99.9% of their DNA, so it begs the questions: Why are we told to feed them so differently, and why are we told that if we do feed them closer to wolf diets, it's bad for them or will make them sick? Wouldn't the inverse be true? (Wayne & Ostrander, 2007). I can't think of any positive answers on this one, so I'll press on.

There is research on this as well, but not necessarily for the purposes of this book. If you want to know which dogs still run incredibly close to the wolf's genetic makeup, it's fun to look up, and the results are surprising. I am sure you have heard that dogs have been domesticated, so raw meat is bad for them. Have you ever stopped to think what domesticated means? Well, it just means to tame or to make a pet, so that argument has no basis either and is irrelevant to their biological makeup, which includes their digestive tract.

Rotational feeding helps create a healthier, optimized digestive system and nutritional variety for your dog. Species appropriate feeding can strengthen your dog's digestive system by introducing a variety of foods in their diet, making it less challenging for them to digest new proteins and minimizing the occurrence of stomach upsets (Kim, 2019).

Implementing a "plant day" and a "meat day" (on separate days, of course) is an example of rotational feeding, or what we call a natural species appropriate diet. This helps ensure that incompatible meals will not meet each other in your dog's digestive tract. It creates space and margins for healing and health to flourish in between, so neither toxicity nor fodder for parasites is created.

Feeding your dog different single kinds of food on different days looks like this (in no particular order):

- meat day
- plant day (aka fruit and veggie day in limited raw amounts)
- fasting day

How could you create your own diet plan that looks like this based on what your dog likes? Let's look! I have created some easy-to-follow examples for you. They give you a starting point to see if your pet likes them so you can also easily tailor to fit your pet's needs and your schedule. So, when you're first starting, it's best to follow a day-by-day chart that outlines everything for you, so you can get the right percentages of plant, meat, or fasting. Once you have implemented the schedule and feel confident about using it, feel free to mix it up while keeping the feeding in a species appropriate format. It will be easy to memorize at that point. For example, when I first started feeding, I was trying to reverse two to three incredibly terrible disease states. I strictly fed my dog fruit for the first few months. I also did a few three-day fasts to create autophagy. I did this before feeding any meat, organs, and vegetables. I worked in meats first, and then organs, since I was already feeding fruits. My dog does enjoy the occasional raw beets or carrots infrequently, as he grew up eating them for snacks before I knew better.

What I fed him was based on the level of healing I observed, from literally looking at my dog. My daily strategies did not come out of a book or program. It was my observation of his hair growing out by more than an inch and a half, which was more than he ever had before in his lifetime, from zero to eleven years old. This showed me he previously was not receiving the proper nutrition or was not even healthy enough to grow a healthy coat for his body. This is why observing your pet is so important. It literally is what allowed me to know that I was on the right track and that my dog was truly healing from the inside out. When you can observe your pet on a daily basis and watch them actually heal, you know you've finally gotten it right. It's an amazing feeling. The problems that you're having with your pet that you think are aging or people have told you are aging, you'll physically see them reverse if the pet has enough vital force to heal.

As you grow in your expertise around species appropriate feeding, you'll be able to randomly feed and not be restricted to a specific pattern. It will turn out super flexible, super easy, and super quick the more you do it. You can even just use what you have in the house at the moment. You will also learn how to stock foods and prep foods for the week in advance to make it super snappy and fun. When I see my dog as happy as he is, it gives me so much joy. And it gives him joy too! I know this because he yells with enthusiasm for every single meal. Knowing that what I'm feeding him is completely allowing him to live a full and vibrant healthy life is priceless. His happiness always makes me happy too!

It comes down to which plan you decide works for you and is most user-friendly for you and most beneficial for your dog, and what your dog likes to eat, because I suggest letting them choose. This was a fun part for me as I tried many foods to vary them and see what he liked most. I changed my diet as well, eating whatever he didn't. So, we now share most everything like we used to, but in a whole, nutritious, disease-preventing, and healthy beneficial way, which feels good for me and him.

How do plant days work? You have options. You are free to combine different types of fruits and vegetables together into single meals. My dog prefers that I feed him one category at a time. He is one of those dogs who does not like different foods in the same plate touching each other. I always stick with his wisdom. The other option is that you can do one day for fruits and a different day for a vegetable. Personally, I have never seen my dog have any problems when I have mixed fruits and certain small amounts of raw veggies together. The overall goal is to never mix carbohydrates (plants), proteins (meats), and never serve too much cellulose (plants). I keep days separate and for us, it's typically some version of plants, fruits, limited raw vegetables and meat and meat items, with fasting weekly.

How Do You Decide How Much to Feed?

Quality matters. So does quantity! Besides the distinctions of what category to feed your dog and the different days to rotate, there's also the important topic of how much to feed her. So, this also makes this topic critical to get a dog's diet fully on point! Overfeeding can enable diseases to get a grip on your dog's body, and much research is out there on the topic of limiting calories. Overeating can diminish her vitality and lifespan, just as it can ours.

If you listen to or follow any so-called gurus in the raw feeding niche, you'll see almost all of them share a breakdown of percentages. These are the guidelines they propose. A blind spot and potential problem is that their guidelines rarely take into account how your dog is different (such as the symptoms he deals with, his breed, how much he weighs, and how much he exercises and at high or low energy levels). Interestingly enough, it's exceptionally difficult to uncover how they made their conclusions. Where's the science and data? It's missing. Doesn't exactly build confidence, does it? Determining what to feed your dog is much easier than understanding and knowing how much to feed her.

As you know, wolves and wild dogs are geared to eat their fill whenever they're given the chance due to food deprivation, which sometimes occurs. No food available? They keep hunting. That's how it works. An adult wolf can consume up to 22 1/2 pounds of meat in one meal, although this is not typical. On the other hand, a wild adult dog can survive for more than 12 days without food (famine), which is part of their natural diet (Kelly, n.d.). That makes up a lot of days for all those pounds of food. What about the average of what they eat? The consumption habits of mature wolves entail an average daily intake of 5 to 14 pounds of meat. Notably, these creatures can endure up to 1.5 to 2 weeks or more without sustenance between feedings. Given that wolves' hunting endeavors result in failure rates ranging from 86% to 97% of the time, they must adhere to a dietary regimen that involves alternating cycles of food scarcity and abundance (Western Wildlife Outreach, n.d.). This also promotes the lack of caloric intake as being beneficial in the long run.

Knowing this information, it's still not possible to know the exact guidelines for our dogs. Here's why. Our dogs are domesticated. They do not have to hunt to survive. In light of that, they're less physically active than wild dogs and wolves. Let's face it. Most of our dogs have easier and cozier lives than we do. As well they should, for all the love and forgiveness they provide!

Furthermore, dogs today are not in tune with how to regulate their intake of food. Their bodies do not live on a feast-or-famine lifestyle.

They can easily overeat and exceed their food intake ... kind of like humans at a mouth-watering buffet. So, it is our job to responsibly observe them and their constitution and adjust food and exercise accordingly. Finally, domestic pet feeds are nowhere near as healthy and clean as the food that nature provides in the wild. All of this tells us we cannot fully and precisely define exactly how much to feed our domesticated dogs based on what we know about wild dogs and wolves.

Truth bomb: There is no expert who can tell you exactly how much food your dog needs to eat. Although they may give you comfort by suggesting blanket statements for "all dogs," the reality is that guidelines are starting points.

Feeding your dog between 2% and 4% of their body weight is commonly shared online. To maintain a healthy weight, dogs typically require 2-4% of their body weight in daily meals, with variance based on energy and activity levels. If your pet is carrying extra weight, consider feeding them closer to 2% of their body weight and encouraging more exercise (Raw and Fresh, 2020).

At first glance, it's easy to feel you know what to do, and that's that. There's more going on here than what you see at first sight. This percentage is almost always based on feeders who follow the PMR method (Prey Model Raw). Meaning, they are feeding their dogs meat every single day. This is different from what I'm suggesting. With a species appropriate diet, your dog will also be eating fruits, plants, and limited raw vegetables and have a fasting day. This creates more of a margin and peace of mind because you will not have to be concerned with your dog eating too much fat. Just as in humans, it's difficult to overeat (overfeed) on plant foods compared to protein-packed cuts of meat. It's possible to feed your dog up to 5% of their body weight on certain days, depending on how many plant days and meat days you do.

Ultimately, percentages are not inherently bad. It's just that you must take note to only view them as a starting point. They are nothing more and nothing less. For anything we measure, we must have a starting point. It's the same thing with our GPS systems in our vehicles. For example, if you want to go somewhere else, you must know from where you are starting, just as a percentage point can easily give us a clear starting point to feed our dogs. Just remember, starting points are not points to maintain in the face of observing something contradictory (i.e., appropriate body weight).

From there, it's your responsibility to observe your dog as I mentioned earlier. Play the role of an observer by watching for any weight gain, detoxing symptoms, and anything out of the ordinary. You will adjust your plant days and meat days. The goal is to optimize your dog's health, and those course-corrections allow you to do that. By taking the time to prepare homemade dog food, you are fostering a closer bond with your furry friend than the brief moments it takes to serve commercial pet feed. This positive change benefits both you and your dog.

What if I make a mistake? You may be asking yourself that question. First, give yourself some grace and patience. I commend you on being open minded to learn this information for yourself and take control of your pet's health and wellness. Doing the exact same for yourself is equally empowering. You're learning something new. It will take some time. Ultimately, it will be worth it. Second, if you're going to make a mistake, let it be slightly underfeeding. If moderate or severe underfeeding goes on for more than a short period of time, it can have dire results. Balance is key, as is moderation. Overfeeding can have bad consequences in the long term, and sometimes, as your dog is healing, it will cause them to regurgitate the amount that simply cannot fit in his belly. This happened with my boy at times; luckily, I figured it out fast. Also, make sure you're feeding room-temperature or cooler food, as warm or hot food can also cause regurgitation with some sensitive dogs like mine. As we have learned, underfeeding is more in line with nature. It will, at worst, probably produce a whiny or upset dog. Can you relate? We all get cranky when we are hungry.

So, if you're feeding your dog correctly, how will you know if you're feeding him the right quantity of food? The answer is found in whether your dog is showing health symptoms. Symptoms are evidence that the quantity is incorrect and off. A lack of symptoms is reason to treat yourself to something nice for being such a phenomenal dog owner!

Let's say you're starting with 3% body weight as the food portion. You see symptoms in your dog. If that happens, you want to reduce the amount of food. You could try 2.5% or 2%, and then observe her. When correcting food percentages, it's always best to start with half an ounce or an ounce. Even that can remedy an issue. At times, it may be that only the amount of fat needs to be reduced, especially if you're not removing the skin and visible fat on meat items. Once again, you're playing the role of chef and logical observer to see what optimizes your dog's health.

What About Balanced Diets and Nutrition?

At this point in the process, what comes up most is the question about nutrients. If you're only looking at quantity, does that mean it's possible for your dog to become nutrient-deficient? The answer is no. In each single food, the energy potential and nutrients are proportional. If the dog does not need the calories, why would she need the nutrients of any food that has been lessened? Put your mind at rest that the healthy feeding you do will provide all the nutrients your dog needs. Even with what I just said, some pet owners will still worry about the quantity and quality of nutrients. This is probably because the commercialized dog feed industry has heavily advertised "Nutrients! Nutrients!" for years now. The worry shows up like "Is my dog getting enough nutrients?" While you're reading this book, you're probably asking yourself, *Will my dog get sufficient nutrients from the specific diet this book promotes?* The answer is yes.

Both dogs and humans need six essential nutrients to function properly. The six major nutrients, in no particular order, are:

1. Carbohydrates
    + Carbohydrates are macronutrients. They consist of sugars, starches, and fibers found in various foods such as fruits, grains, vegetables, and dairy products. Despite being criticized in some popular diets, carbohydrates are essential for maintaining a healthy diet as they are one of the fundamental food groups (Szalay, 2021).
    + To stay in a species appropriate diet, in nature, wolves and wild dogs only eat on average 4% to 8% carbohydrates. This is based on Stadler indicating earlier that 8% comes from berries and grasses, which are carbs (Stahler, et al., 2006). Note that these come from plants and fruits, not grains or other foods high in starch, like potatoes, rice, and corn. Eggs, fish, plants, vegetables, insects, and fruits generally contain an average of 4% starch and sugar content. Non-sugar and non-starch carbs, proteins, fiber, and fats make up the remaining 96% (Patton, 2013).

- The reason is that dogs have eight hormones that raise blood sugar, and only one that lowers it (insuline). What this means is on the rare occasion that they have eaten too many carbs, then there is a hormone there to lower blood sugar. Conversely, the other seven hormones are there to raise blood sugar because starch is not normally part of their diet (Patton, 2013).
2. Fats (lipids)
   - Fats are another macronutrient. Proper intake of dietary fat, both in terms of quantity and quality, is crucial for maintaining optimal health (Szalay, 2015). Dietary fats can be categorized as saturated (found in butter, cheese, meat), polyunsaturated (found in fish oil, flaxseed oil, sunflower oil), or monounsaturated (found in olive oil) (Savory Prime Pet, n.d.). On this diet, the goal is to feed small amounts of fat.
3. Proteins
   - Proteins are the third and final macronutrient. Protein consists of amino acids, which are commonly called the building blocks of life. They assist with bones, skin, nails, and muscles. Proteins are vital for producing hormones, neurotransmitters, enzymes, and antibodies to maintain optimal body function. Essential amino acids are required in a dog's diet as their body cannot generate them in adequate amounts. In the absence of sufficient carbohydrates and fats, proteins can also provide energy. As the body cannot store protein, it needs a continuous supply from the diet (Savory Prime Pet, n.d.).
4. Minerals
   - Minerals are a requirement for both human and animal life. Minerals branch into two categories. The first is

macro-minerals, which include calcium, phosphorus, potassium, sodium, and magnesium. They play important roles in various bodily functions such as building strong bones, regulating fluid balance, transmitting nerve impulses, and maintaining a healthy heartbeat. The second category is trace minerals (or trace elements), which include iron, zinc, manganese, and others. These minerals help support the body's immune system, maintain healthy bones and teeth, and facilitate a wide range of enzymatic reactions in the body. (Australian Fitness Academy, 2019).

5. Vitamins
   + Vitamins are essential micronutrients. Both humans and dogs need these in small quantities. They allow the metabolism to function properly. Like minerals, vitamins must come from food. Vitamins have important functions in the body, such as regulating calcium and phosphorus levels (vitamin D), strengthening the immune system (vitamin A), acting as antioxidants (vitamin C and E), aiding blood clotting (vitamin K), and supporting nervous system function (vitamin B12) (Savory Prime Pet, n.d.).

6. Water
   + Like humans, a dog's body is close to 80% water. Without water, there can be no life. Water has several crucial roles in the body, such as facilitating the transportation of nutrients to cells and their dissolution, regulating body temperature, aiding in the digestion of protein, fat, and carbohydrates, cushioning organs and the nervous system, and eliminating waste from the body (Savory Prime Pet, n.d.).

What's the difference between macronutrients and micronutrients? Macronutrients are essential nutrients required in relatively larger quantities by the body, including carbohydrates, proteins, and fats, which serve as the primary source of energy for the body. Micronutrients, on the other hand, are nutrients needed in smaller amounts and include vitamins and minerals (Get Smarter, 2020).

When it comes to nutrients, it's not about ingredient requirements. The focus should be on specific nutrient requirements. Dogs need certain nutrients instead of feedstuffs (National Research Council, 2006). Feedstuffs is a food provided for cattle and other livestock. What your dog needs is naturally contained in the diet described in this book. You do not need to add anything chemical, toxic, or human-made. The diet this book advocates for will help provide your dog with a sufficient amount of quality macronutrients and micronutrients. Rest assured, this diet is a healthy and holistic choice for your dog.

If you want more details about the exact nutrient levels of each food you're going to feed, check out the USDA food calculator online, called FoodData Central Search Results (U.S. Department of Agriculture, n.d.). It is listed in the references if you'd like to use it directly in the ebook through the hyperlink. It gives a precise nutrient amount, by ounce, for any type of food. https://fdc.nal.usda.gov/fdc-app.html#/?query=food%20calculator.

If you want additional information on nutrition profiles, there is an organization called AAFCO. They set the standards for pet food and what makes it complete and balanced. They are not concerned about species-appropriate foods or bioavailability. Their standards allow for the destruction of enzymes through high temperature processing. They allow for high amounts of carbs, using synthetic vitamins and minerals and rancid fatty acids. They also allow genetically modified meat and veggies, as well as hormones, chemicals and pesticides. None of this has to be disclosed on the labels. So, you may want to consider not getting your nutrition profiles from there. I listed this because it's what everyone talks about.

There is another nutrition organization called WSAVA Global Veterinary Community who set global guidelines for nutrition for pets. They offer expert-based nutrition information for companion animals to veterinarians to support veterinary healthcare teams.

What Are Some Cost-Cutting Strategies to Get the Best Foods at the Best Prices?

Depending on the size of your dog and if you have more than one, cost plays out in different ways. For small dogs, you will spend less, or you can spend the same as you would on a big dog (possibly) if buying the highest quality of foods. It's your choice. If you have a large dog or two or more, your monthly cost will likely be a bigger consideration.

TIP 3

Here are tips to keep your dog(s) healthy without breaking the bank:

- Watch online and for paper supermarket advertisements and visit the store websites for e-coupons.

- Look online for companies that sell ugly organic fruits and vegetables at a discounted rate.

- Stock up on foods (especially frozen and whole chickens) when they're on sale.

- Check with local farmers.

- Ask your supermarket butcher section or store manager if they sell frozen turkey scrap or chicken scrap. (Usually these are the backs and necks, FYI.)

- Sometimes super-high-quality organic farmers sell internal organs that aren't normally put up for sale, but if you call, you may be able to buy.

- For fruits and plants, ask supermarket or produce managers if they have overripe and perishable fruits and plants that you can have.

- Visit Asian markets and ask about chicken frames and fish scraps to see what's available.

- Look for small game hens at Target or Walmart along with other supermarkets.

- Review Facebook Marketplace, Craigslist, and similar sites for freezer clean-outs.

- Consider what's available in your area in different seasons. Rural locations may offer something that's not available in cities, and vice versa. For example, see if emu scrap is available where you live. It's usually budget-friendly.

- Look for online co-ops that focus on raw feeding.

- Explore the possibilities of connecting one on one with local farmers, butchers, and similar professionals.

- Ask other raw feeders in your area or region where they buy their food.

- Facebook raw or holistic groups are also a good source to see where they get their foods.

With a little attention and focus and a little prepping, it's possible to feed your dog healthy foods without going over your monthly budget or taking extra time. You may even save money! How cool is that? Another factor that helps your budget is that my suggested plan for your dog is species appropriate. This approach has a factor in helping people I coach stay on or under budget. Once you get in the zone, it goes easier and faster than what you'd expect. An important related topic is organic versus free range. The cost differences cannot be ignored. Let's look at the differences first. With chickens, for example, the main focus is about what the chickens eat. On standard free-range farms, anything goes with feeding. Organic farms are required to use synthetic and chemical-free non-GMO feeds. Hens on organic farms are only allowed to consume pure organic feed and are prohibited from consuming animal byproducts such as eggshells and ground bones to be considered officially organic (Foundation Education, 2018). Furthermore, the term "organic" pertains to a group of regulations established by the government that emphasizes avoiding the use of synthetic substances and food for organic animals, as well as requiring a minimum amount of outdoor access. In contrast, "free-range" only refers to the animals having access to the outdoors and does not address the sources of food or use of chemicals (Zvi, n.d.).

My first recommendation is organic, if possible. As I wrote previously, organic helps us avoid GMOs, pesticides, and accounts for nutritional density. However, a dog can still do very well on non-organic food. When trying to reverse disease, it's a better choice to use the organic nutrient levels and less toxic chemicals, etc. Ultimately, you can feed your dog:

1. organic,
2. free range, or
3. both.

As for context, keep in mind that free-range animals are a business. Every business aims to keep their costs down. This means they are raising those animals and feeding them as cheaply as possible. Because of this, free-range animals are less healthy. They're also fatter. Why? Because they're most likely eating processed junk, garbage, or GMO grains.

With free range, I recommend trimming off fat because that's where the toxins are mostly stored! How great is it that you can basically cut off the toxic part? Don't be shy. Trim fat off if you purchase free range. The more fat trimmed, the more toxins removed. Just as in humans, animals store toxins in their fat. If we are eating fat, we are eating the toxins they had in their bodies. Kind of freaky, right? Using plant days instead of daily meat with a species appropriate diet has another benefit. Plant days are low fat!

This means your dog's total consumption of fat will be low.

Meat animals naturally raised are given more appropriate foods to eat. Still, trim off the fat. Finally, never feed your dog ground meat. It does not matter if it's beef, chicken, or something else. You never want to feed your dog ground meats because it's impossible to trim out the fat. Ground meat is what it is, and there's no controlling your dog's fat intake when you feed it to him, thus you lose the ability to control toxins in fat.

Two meats that make for healthy and nutritious meals are quail and game hens. They do cost more. However, they are ideal foods for your dog. Their bone-to-meat breakdown is similar to that of wild prey. Keep in mind that both bones and meat are equally important.

You may still be concerned about the raw feeding financial costs. I totally get it. Overall, your cost should be lower, if not the same. Consider the cost breakdowns of commercialized versus raw feeding: the total includes your average number of yearly trips to the vet, the commercialized pet feed, any treats you usually purchase, major illnesses possibly due to traditional feeding, and so on. I would recommend you stop reading the book now, get out a piece of paper and pen, and take fifteen minutes to add up your costs. By doing so, you will have a clear and accurate picture of what you are paying now and after implementing this diet.

Although raw feeding costs will vary depending on the size of your dog and the options you choose to keep your costs down that I highlighted earlier, here's some helpful information.

One popular website calculated that the average cost of feeding a grain-free diet to a 50-pound dog per day is $1.66. Switching to feeding your dog 100% real food, the daily cost increases by $2.38. If you have a smaller dog, like a 26-pound Parson Jack Russell for example, the increase was only $1.19 more per day (Steve's Real Food, 2015). Of course, this varies depending on if you buy in bulk or do individual meals versus meal preparation in bulk.

TIP 4

The Raw Feeding Community website did a study of 224 dog owners. Here is what they learned about the average costs per pound for raw pet food:

Less than $.50: 1.8%
$.50 to a $1.00: 7.6%
$1.00 to $1.50: 33.9%
$1.50 to $2.00: 33.5%
$2.00 to $2.50: 14.3%
$2.50 to $3.00: 4%
Greater than $3.00: 4.9%

(How Much Does It Cost To Feed Raw? 2019)

The following computations represent the last stage in determining the required amount of food for a duration of one month (30 days) and may serve as a basis for additional calculations. Upon obtaining the monthly aggregates, an average rate per pound (or kilogram) can be employed to arrive at a monthly approximation. For individuals residing in the continental United States, it is suggested to utilize a cost of $2.50 per pound, whereas for other nations, a cost of $6 per kilogram is recommended, although this amount may differ due to currency exchange rates.

Multiplying 30 by $2.50 results in a monthly budget of $75, using an average cost of $2.50 per pound. Similarly, multiplying 13.59 by $6 gives a monthly budget of $81.54, using an average cost of $6 per kilogram (Perfectly Rawsome Website, n.d.). To find out how to feed your dog, see chapter 8 for the calculations.

With a little elbow grease, asking around, and by implementing my recommendations from earlier, I'm convinced you can maintain a budget of $30 to $60 per month. Keep in mind that you're not feeding your dog meat every day, and this instantly lowers the overall cost. Veggies and fruits are cheaper. Don't forget that adding de-saponified quinoa (flakes) and millet will further lower your costs. Plus, every fasting day is a $0 cost day. Unless you have two or more large dogs, raw feeding is almost always more budget-friendly. Before I transitioned my dog to this diet, my average cost was about $350 to $400 per month with supplements and the best commercialized organic dog food and supplemental feeding, special dog bones, and so on. On top of that, I used organic vegetables in the afternoon as snacks prior to finding, researching, and implementing the diet you're reading about here.

Finally, do not forget the other costs of a traditional convenience-driven pet feed. When you have a sick dog, it's not only costing you money; it's costing you time, physical energy, and emotional energy. You can either choose to pay money to keep them healthy or to have drugs and surgeries to keep them around, which is the same for people. In my case in the past, it also caused major stress. It was super scary and stressful! It's always so heart-heavy when we're up late trying to sleep but can't because we're worried about the dogs we love so much. I know it earned me a lot of extra gray hairs. Sometimes, we find ourselves in a vet facility under massive testing for 12 hours, only to return there again a day or two later. One time, I drove over three hours one way for the best testing available. Sounds like a recipe for exhaustion, doesn't it? How about we lower your stress and costs while optimizing your dog's health? Keep reading.

Should You Cut the Meat or Not? Does It Matter?

It's not your job officially to cut the meat like a super-chef. Your job is to place out the meat as intact and whole as you can. Give your dog the opportunity to cut and tear their own food. Let him use his instincts. Doing it this way allows her to put her cutting teeth into action, making the meat into regular bite-size portions that's best for her. A huge benefit is that it gives your dog's digestive tract sufficient time to prepare to receive the food, which will arrive quickly. Also, it maintains teeth being cleaned and reduces tartar. Does cutting the meat make his or her bowl and surrounding area less messy? Yes. However, that's an owner-convenience viewpoint. I invite you to do what's best for your dog. The exception, of course, is if your dog is a gulper.

Some dog owners are concerned about giving their dogs big cuts of meat and bone. The reason for this is their dogs tend to wolf down or gulp their food immediately. You need to know this is rarely the case. When gulping does occur, concern is warranted. If your dog throws up after gulping and swallowing his food super-fast, that would be a sign that you need to take a different direction or action.

Chewing food is an important part of the digestion process. When dogs eat too quickly, it can result in various digestive issues, including vomiting and gastric dilation, which is a serious condition that can be life-threatening. In addition to the potential health problems, speed eating can also lead to choking and gagging. Therefore, it is important to take steps to slow down a dog's eating habits to ensure optimal digestive health and reduce the risk of these serious conditions (London, 2016).

In this instance, usually the best solution is to hand-feed your dog slowly. For example, you may have to spend time holding a chicken leg. This way, you can teach him to eat slowly. If that fails, a different option is to use a dog bowl designed to slow down eating speed. These have several names, including eat slow bowl, dog pause bowl, eat slower pet dish, etc. They're easy to find in stores and online. If an eat slow bowl does not work, you may have to cut the meat into smaller pieces or grind it. The great majority have no issues, even those dogs with less teeth. Again, observe your dog for safety. You want to feel comfortable that they have learned what they need to do.

When it comes to cutting meat or not, goat meat is in its own category. Always cut goat meat. Here's why. It has a coarser texture. If you've ever eaten it, you know it's very sinewy. Sinew is a piece of tough fibrous tissue. Its job is to connect muscle to bone or bone to bone. They're also known as tendons or ligaments. It's possible your dog will swallow before she cuts or tears the meat. Remember when you were a kid and swallowed a spaghetti noodle, but half went down your esophagus and the other half was in your mouth? It's like that, except with goat meat, it can cause choking. That's why it's always best to cut goat meat to be on the safe side.

In this book, I talk about a variety of foods. If goats are not common in your region, don't worry about it. That goes for all of the foods covered in this book. I write about many types of foods from all over the world to give numerous examples. This does not mean you must feed a certain item if it's not in your region, or if it's a food that is too large or small for your dog.

When you need to cut meat, cut it:

1. big enough so that it's impossible to swallow without chewing, or
2. little enough to swallow without the need to chew.

Finally, when you feed your dog bones, my advice is to watch him eat. At the very least, stay in the same area. Safety matters. You can also break up bones with meat knives if you choose. There are ones that look a lot like medieval cleavers. Those will break up a bone. If you do not have one, a hammer can work (although it is not my main recommendation). It's always best to use tools designed for their specific purposes.

Does the temperature of the raw meat matter? If your dog got to decide, she would pick eating meat at body temperature. It's fine to let meat sit out a while so it can get to room or body temperature prior to feeding. Regardless, they will be thrilled to eat cold food, too, whether it's meat, veggies, or fruit. Both body temperature and room temperature will work fine. My dog prefers cool and fresh. Dogs have their own preferences, so try them and observe. Your dog will tell you which is his favorite. Of course, some dogs are more opinionated than others. Mine has a real mind of his own, which I love!

Is Bone Really Safe? Dispelling the Controversy.

Cooked bones are not safe. Raw bones are safe, although it does depend on the size of your dog. Bones should be matched to the size of the dog.

Logically speaking, a small dog cannot be expected to eat a really hard or big bone. It's best to use common sense in this area when choosing bone sizes and types.

As I wrote earlier, cooking bones and meat diminishes their healthy properties and changes the structure of the bone to inorganic. Bones can become devoid of nutrition. At times, they can become dangerous for dogs to eat once cooked, as they get brittle. This can splinter and cause shards (AKC Staff, 2020). Swallowing shards can cause a blockage and other gastrointestinal issues for your dog.

Health benefits are quite abundant with raw bones, though, and they are needed for proper nutrition, as we learned in Chapter 5.

- Bones offer various benefits for dogs' behavior, health, and nutrition. Dogs tend to love bones as the anticipation of eating them releases dopamine, which has a soothing and calming effect on dogs. Chewing on bones encourages natural behavior in dogs. In terms of health, bones help maintain healthy teeth and gums by providing fresh calcium for strong bones. They also act as roughage for healthy digestion, promoting bright white teeth and healthy gums. In addition, bones offer various nutrients such as fresh marrow, zinc, selenium, magnesium, and boost immunity. They provide proper minimal fats and vitamins for vitality and contain glucosamine and chondroitin, which promote healthy joints in dogs (Dogs First, n.d.).

- My dog loves to lick and chew. Since dogs have different personalities and preferences, how they respond to bones will vary.

- It's understandable that the thought of our dog(s) eating bones can be a bit unnerving, depending on how much one knows. It's not so unnerving for an informed dog owner, as you have now learned. Always be cautious and keep an eye on them just like you do with toys. It's not wise to leave your dog home alone with toys available or in reach. They can choke on those just as easily as dangerous bones.

- Another helpful fact to know is that certain teeth in dogs are called carnassial teeth. These teeth are designed to easily slice through meat, cartilage, and bone. These teeth are found in all carnivorous animals, but the carnassial teeth of dogs are especially powerful. It is easy to recognize that dogs are more than capable of eating bones (Dogs First, n.d.). The fourth premolars of a dog's upper jaw house the powerful carnassial teeth, which are considerably bigger than the other teeth. Their unique structure and size allow them to crush and grind tough foods with ease (Covetrus: North America, 2016).

You'll truly be impressed if this is the first time you see your dog eat bones! I certainly was. I felt that I really underestimated my wild boy! It was amazing! I realized how similar to wild dogs they really are, even after we have domesticated them so much ... even down to those wearing adorable designer dog outfits!

Additionally, bones fully dissolve in the stomachs of dogs due to their digestive juices. They have very strong stomach acids because they are built to eat items like bones with ease. The acids also increase the ease of digestion. While bones are certainly dangerous for humans, dogs' bodies are designed to consume raw bones. For further reading, you can check out *Give Your Dog a Bone*, written by Dr. Ian Billinghurst. He is a Doctor of Veterinary Medicine.

How do you choose the right bone to start with and progress to them comfortably eating them if they did not learn from puppyhood? Here's a great breakdown.

Selecting the appropriate bone size for your dog is crucial to determine their chewing behavior. When in doubt, choose a bigger bone to be safe. Once you understand your dog's preferences, you can switch to smaller sizes. It is recommended to give stick-shaped bones like turkey necks or beef ribs to first-time bone chewers like puppies, holding one end while letting them chew on the other end. As a responsible dog owner, it is essential to monitor your dog while chewing bones, preventing them from swallowing the whole bone. Overconsumption of bones can cause hard and chalky stools. Sometimes, loose stools may be a result if the bone is too rich. Adding pumpkin to your dog's meal can help regulate digestion if they eat too much bone. To prevent overconsumption, it is advisable to give bones in multiple sittings (True Carnivores, n.d.).

Have a puppy? If so, watch her because eating too much bone can lead to constipation. The easiest measure is to give the amount of bone that matches the portions from the animal you're feeding. For example, if you want to give your pup a chicken quarter, include that bone from that portion.

Here are some helpful tips from Dog Time: It is important to closely monitor your dog while they are chewing on a bone to prevent potential choking or injury from aggressive gnawing. Any bones that have been chewed down to a brittle state should be thrown away, as they pose a risk of splintering or becoming a choking hazard if further gnawed down. It is also crucial to assess your dog's chewing habits before giving them bones, as dogs who tend to bite off large chunks or swallow food quickly may be at a higher risk of harm. To reduce this risk, bones should be given with meat and should be longer than the length of your dog's muzzle to prevent them from being swallowed whole. Additionally, avoid giving your dog bones that are cut lengthwise or are more prone to splintering, such as pork or rib bones (Clark, n.d.).

Finally, always avoid what is called weight-bearing bones of larger animals, like cows. They're dangerous for dogs because they are highly dense and strong. They can possibly break teeth, especially for smaller size dogs. These bones may be referred to as any of the following: femurs, thigh bones, pet bones, and marrow bones.

CHAPTER 7

What Types of Foods Do Most People Feed on a Species Appropriate Diet?

WHEN IT COMES DOWN TO Species Appropriate Feeding, there are only three kinds of food and one category of abstaining/fasting:

1. meats
2. plants (fruits, vegetables fed sparingly, mixed plants)
3. fasting

As you learned earlier, the goal is that meats and plants never "meet," touch, or combine in your dog's stomach. When they do, implement number three above—fasting. The margin between the meat feedings and plant feedings, along with fasting day, can help create the magic! In this context, by magic I'm talking about vitality, energy, health, and a long lifespan for your dog. If that's not magical and exciting, I don't know what is.

Therapeutic fasting and calorie-restricted diets are advantageous for both humans and dogs, especially in terms of increasing life expectancy. Therapeutic fasting is generally defined as abstaining from all foods and only drinking pure water for a certain amount of time (Scanlan, 2011). It's important to know that not everyone defines therapeutic fasting the same way, as some people may allow for tea, soups, fruits, etc. What are calorie-restricted diets? Calorie restriction is a type of diet that focuses on eating fewer calories than you or your pet normally would. It is based on the idea that reducing calorie intake can lead to a longer, healthier life. This is because it forces the body to use its stored energy reserves, which may aid in reducing the likelihood of age-related diseases and serve to decelerate the aging process (Scanlan, 2011). It's important to note that both therapeutic fasting and calorie-restricted diets include getting the necessary nutrients the body needs.

Reducing calorie intake to 60-70% of the necessary amount required for adult weight maintenance has been shown to increase the lifespan of various species by 30-50%, as well as bestowing excellent health benefits. This approach has been observed across a broad range of species (Johnson et al., 2006).

The practice of alternate day calorie restriction involves having no less of a calorie intake of 50% to 80% of the estimated daily requirement on one day, followed by a day of normal eating. In as little as two weeks, improvements in health conditions can be observed such as insulin resistance, seasonal allergies, asthma, and infectious diseases that originated from bacteria, viruses and fungi (Johnson et al., 2006).

What can calorie restriction look like for people and canines? In the case of humans, a varied diet consisting of numerous nutrient-rich raw foods, particularly fruits, leafy greens, nuts, seeds, and vegetables, is recommended. As for animals, research on calorie-restriction suggests limiting their food intake to 70% of what the control animals are consuming. Even in the absence of increasing the nutrient density, these animal studies indicate that health improves, degenerative diseases are less prevalent, and lifespan is prolonged (Scanlan, 2011).

Research suggests that high-calorie diets and a lack of folic acid may increase the risk of developing Alzheimer's and Parkinson's disease. Animal studies have demonstrated that reducing calorie intake or intermittent fasting and adding folic acid to the diet can decrease neuronal damage and improve behavior. These positive effects seem to be due to an increase in neurotrophic factors and cytoprotective protein chaperones in neurons resulting from dietary restriction. Additionally, folic acid can help prevent DNA damage in neurons caused by homocysteine and oxidative stress, while also protecting cerebral vessels. While further studies are needed to determine the effectiveness of these dietary interventions in humans, the available evidence suggests that high-calorie diets and elevated homocysteine levels may make the brain more susceptible to neurodegenerative disorders related to aging, especially when someone is genetically predisposed (Mattson, 2003).

What is oxidative stress? Oxidative stress is a condition in which a body experiences an imbalance between the production and elimination of free radicals. As you know, free radicals are unstable atoms that harm cells and ultimately cause diseases, if not countered by antioxidants. What does this have to do with aging? A lot!

Many age-related diseases and the aging process itself are thought to be caused by oxidative stress. Calorie restriction has been shown to slow down these negative age-related processes. Current research indicates that calorie restriction can help regulate the body's redox environment and provide antioxidant protection, thereby slowing down the aging process (Kim et al., 2002).

Another benefit of fasting is that it allows the liver to completely process released waste products. The liver will take one of two actions. It will either evacuate the waste products through bile, or it will release them into the bloodstream so the kidneys can eliminate them. The miracle of this is that it decreases the toxic load the body was carrying.

It has been researched that fasting for a period of 48 hours or more can protect normal cells from the harmful effects of chemotherapy. As a result, this method has been utilized in some human chemotherapy patients to alleviate the adverse effects of treatment. It is worth considering implementing this technique in companion animals suffering from cancer. Furthermore, numerous investigations have observed that an increased lifespan can be attained in various organisms, such as mice, rhesus monkeys, and Labrador retrievers (Scanlan, 2011).

As you know, the source of many degenerative diseases is inflammation. A calorie-restricted diet also shows evidence for:

- decreasing occurrences of cancer (Fontana et al., 2010) (Longo & Fontana 2010)

- decreasing high blood pressure (Gláucia et al., 2010)

- reversing Type 2 diabetes (Perry et al., 2017) (Kashef, 2017)

- reducing dermatitis (Perkins et al., 1998)

- decreasing arthritis (Mlacnik et al., 2006)

- increasing cognitive health (Mattson, 2003) (Witte et al., 2009

You may worry about your dog fasting. However, consider wild dogs and wolves for a moment. They are adapted to feast or famine. It's normal for them. Fasting, though not by choice, is a common circumstance in their lives. Whether they're experiencing a time of famine or a period of eating here and there, the reduced calories are actually beneficial to their health. As you know, your dog is a descendant of wolves, and giving their digestive tract even a 24-hour fast to heal can be incredibly beneficial. Some studies suggest that autophagy can be initiated in cells after a period of 24 to 48 hours of fasting (Cleveland Clinic).

Although there is a lot of research that shows the positive effects and value of fasting and calorie restriction for both humans and our beloved canines, sometimes people shy away from it and they really shouldn't. When you're trying to reverse entrenched disease states, fasting can really be beneficial. Given the evidence, it is easy to see that everything that goes on and in your dog greatly matters.

What Vegetables Can You Feed Your Dog that You Probably Should Not Because They're Not Necessarily Species Appropriate?

Veggies that dogs can typically eat easily but should be limited to small amounts include carrots, jicama and cruciferous veggies. (Note:

Although most people think squash and peppers are vegetables, they are actually fruits.)

Potatoes are a bit problematic when compared to the other types of veggies. In light of that, I avoid using them. Can your dog eat a baked potato? Yes. Is it in her best interest? No. What about raw potatoes? Both WebMD and American Kennel Club advise against feeding your dog raw potatoes.

Not easily found in all parts of the U.S., jicama is a root vegetable that is most common in Mexico and Central America. It has an 8.0 pH, which makes it alkaline (HEALable, 2020). Although it is starchy, it is safe for your dog to eat raw jicama. Never feed jicama leaves to your dog, as they are toxic. Just so you know, I've purchased many jicamas in different stores, and I've never seen any with leaves, but it is possible you will come across them.

Cruciferous veggies are next. These options for your dog include:

1. broccoli (sometimes causes gas)
2. Brussels sprouts (sometimes causes gas in certain dogs)
3. cauliflower (sometimes causes gas in certain dogs and it can be painful)
4. green beans

TIP 5

One tip is to not mix these with any other foods at first. You want to see if your dog will eat them as they are. Can you combine them with other plant foods later on in the nutrition plan? Yes, you can! Feel free to get a little creative, too, once you know your dog likes them. Do not try to hide them in meals. Let your dog choose what they enjoy!

What Are Good Fruits for Dogs?

First of all, the main piece of information to know about fruits is that they are primarily composed of simple sugars and water. Most fruits have little to no starch and cellulose. If it were a competition between choosing vegetables or fruits for your dog, the smartest choice every time would be fruits! Most dogs sense this and know it on some level, and that's why they gravitate toward eating fruits over veggies.

One feeding tip is to feed your dog fruits in their natural state. Do not mix or disguise the specific fruit at first. Simply see if she will eat it. When they choose to eat a blueberry, at that moment, they understand it is a food they can eat. Never force foods (fruit or otherwise) on your dog. It's safe to assume that, like people, dogs are also listening to their bodies. Sometimes, they simply know. Force feeding is not a solution. My dog turns his head if he doesn't want something I am offering. My response? I say okay and move on. This is about him, not me. Obviously, during the beginning stage, this will happen. You need to memorize and work your way through menu items that you feel are most nutritious. See which ones your dog enjoys the most. In my case and likely yours, you will come up with the top favorite choices. From there, you can turn them into plant mixtures.

Historically, fruits have been a secondary or backup food. Whenever prey was not an option, the search for fruit was on. Implementing fruit helps mix it up and adds variety to your dog's menu.

Fruits have different categories. There are sweet fruits, neutral fruits, which are known as sub-acidic, and citrus and acidic fruits. For reference, neutral fruits are classified as neutral because they have neither an acidic effect nor an alkaline effect. Sweet and sub-acidic (neutral) fruits your dog can eat include:

- apple
- avocado
- banana
- blueberry
- cucumber
- fig
- mango
- melon
- papaya
- pear
- persimmon

It surprises most people to learn that avocado is a fruit. To be more precise, according to botanists, it is categorized as a large berry that contains only one seed (Bjarnadottir, 2019). Dogs can eat avocados raw. You must remove the outer shell along with the seed inside before feeding. The seed in the center can cause choking, obstruction, and toxicity. Don't feed too much, as it is also considered a fat, a plant fat, but still a fat, which we are trying to reduce overall.

Make sure the fruits you feed your dog are ripe. When you feed your dog bananas, you want them to have brown or black spots.

Citrus and acidic fruits include:

- grapefruit
- orange
- raspberry
- strawberry

After you wash off the fruits, your dog can eat these fruits above as is, unless otherwise noted. Grind, mash, or mush them up so your dog can derive the nutrition from them. Allow your dog to enjoy these yummy meals until their digestive system is healed. However, if you see that your dog's poop has any type of whole fruit, it's best to drop that fruit or veggie from your food list for your dog, or mush it up, so your dog can derive the full nutrition from it. When dogs' gastrointestinal tracts are healing from disease or drugs, mushing up foods for them helps with digestion and nutrient absorption. Again, observation and digestion are the keys. We are what we eat. Like humans, dogs digest and absorb their food. If your dog is not absorbing a specific food, then he or she is also not getting the proper nutrition it offers.

It will come as no surprise that your dog may or may not eat anything on the list of fruits and veggies! Some dogs will devour these foods and others will flat-out refuse to eat them. Just like people, they have their own personalities and preferences. Most of the time, dogs are not interested in citrus and acidic fruits.

What About Foods Used as Protein Substitutes?

Protein substitutes are obviously used as a meat substitute by some dog owners. Historically speaking and based on what you've read here about wolves and wild dogs, you know that eating such meat substitutes is not the norm, nor is it species appropriate. Frankly, we're putting our dogs in a whole new territory biologically with these foods. However, many pet owners are enthusiastic about feeding their dogs vegan or vegetarian nutrition plans because of the results. Sometimes, they get results despite feeding a fully vegan nutrition plan. Is it better than any commercialized pet feed? Absolutely. Is it species appropriate? Not quite. Can they get good results? Yes. However, in the long term, many of the nutrients that dogs need come from internal organs, which are meat-based. Still, from a historical perspective, we must approach these foods with care and caution. I will go over them below in case people still use them. I'm not in support of using them as my stance is that a species appropriate diet is optimal.

Wolves and wild dogs live on prey. To me, this signals that going 100% vegan with your dog is not the best idea. Going vegan with a meat feeding anywhere from three to eight times a month would be more in line with a dog's biology. Frankly, although we have lots of research nowadays, there is no widely agreed-on minimum requirement of meat consumption for dogs. I have a high-energy, high-prey-drive dog. I feed raw meat three times per week, back-to-back, with a 24-hour fast afterward on the third day. Other diets suggest only one to two meat days a week for older dogs. In my situation, it was not enough meat for my dog.

Each dog is different. You must observe. If their muscle isn't where it used to be before they detoxed, or they need more muscle to get back to where they were pre-detox, or need more weight, then you need to add an extra meat day or extra quinoa day. De-saponified quinoa works well for dogs that go through a period where they are really hungry for a bit. It helps them stay feeling fuller longer.

With these foods, you're moving into an area of needing to figure it out yourself through daily observation. You're the one observing your dog. Let me share how to approach this. Let's say you want to implement a nutrition plan that does not feature meat on the menu at all or one that only permits your dog to minimally eat meat. I do not suggest this type of plan based on research, but if you do it, I'll give some guidelines here. So, when you start this new diet plan, you want to be hypervigilant and observant of your dog. Do any symptoms arise? Does anything seem off or different about your dog? If so, you will want to increase the amount of meat on the menu if your dog is experiencing too much weight loss or if you need to slow down his detox symptoms. Meat can be fed to your dog one to two times a week if you want. Some dog owners implement this pattern and have healthy dogs. However, as you know, not all dogs are the same. If, by chance, something negative comes up, you can quickly course-correct by adding more meat or less meat or fasting, so all the dog's energy goes to healing. Fasting will help overcome symptoms more quickly and allow your dog to focus all its body's energy on healing.

What about beans? Your dog can eat cooked beans, but you want to cook the beans well. Don't use salt or any types of flavors. Beans are a complex food high in starch. On a positive note, they are high in protein too. Usually, dogs know they are high-starch unflavored foods, and they avoid beans. Without adding any other foods, put the cooked beans in a bowl in front of your dog. If they eat them, that's great! That shows she understands they are food, and it's a sign they can digest them. However, feeding your dog cooked beans is not species appropriate because of the cooking and because of the item. I would not suggest using them.

As you can imagine, some pet owners, in an effort to outsmart their dog, will disguise the beans (or another food) with other foods so their dog will eat them. Just because a pet owner outsmarts her dog does not mean the action she is taking is smart. There's a case to be made that tricking our dogs into eating food is a bit cruel but also teaches your dog they can't trust you, if they notice (which they likely will). Most things dogs do are related to scent. Hiding a food is likely noticed, even if they eat it. Overall, you want a positive relationship with your dog, especially in tough times. It's best you have an honest and trusting relationship with them. Given how wonderful they are to us and all the joy they bring, it's not just the right thing to do, but at minimum, we owe them that respect.

What about nuts? First of all, a dog is not able to chew nuts adequately. As such, his body cannot absorb the nutrients inside of the nuts. Plus, unless they are soaked or sprouted like beans, they cannot get the nutrients out of them, just like humans cannot. With that knowledge (and without going into it too deeply), view nuts as tasty pleasure-eating for your dog, rather than something nutritious, unless they are soaked and creamed into a butter. Remember, even though they are plants, they still have fat.

Peanuts are often confused with nuts. Although they are called peanuts, they are not actually related to tree nuts. Instead, they belong to the legume family and share ancestry with beans, lentils, and soy (Healthline, n.d.). This explains why their makeup is similar to beans. Overall, when dogs are given the chance to eat smooth-processed cooked peanuts, they enjoy them. We call that peanut butter. If you feed your dog peanuts, only use ones that have no salt and no added oils. It's best to read the labels to verify that there are no toxic ingredients, in addition to the peanuts, which there often can be. I do not feed these types of items because they contain lectins and because they're not species appropriate. I would not feed them. We'll discuss why legumes and grains are mainly nutrient-void in the upcoming lectins section later on.

What about nut butters, like almond butter and peanut butter? If you choose to feed your dog a nut butter, the best choice is raw sprouted almond butter. Sprouting does remove the majority of the lectins to make them more nutritionally available. If you feed your dog peanut butter, purchase a brand that is natural and unsalted. Be sure it does not have hulls or Xylitol added to it. (That goes for anything you feed your dog.) It's okay to offer your dog regular peanut butter as a treat. The ingredient that poses a risk is Xylitol, which is toxic to dogs. It's a sugar substitute sometimes used in reduced-sugar or sugar-free peanut butter. You can safely feed your dog peanut butter as long as it does not have Xylitol (National Peanut Board, n.d.).

A little peanut butter wouldn't be toxic for any healthy dog. For my dog, I choose not to give it, as it has a lot of fat. Also, I'm not a personal fan because of the nutritional value. I definitely don't allow my food likes or dislikes to impact my dog negatively, but I do use the most nutritious foods with the least fat when I offer current or new food choices. I address all foods positively and happily to him. I also feed them to him unless he tells me they are a no-go! My dog has a complete mind of his own and knows precisely what his likes and dislikes are. He is very clear in telling me and there's no mistake about it.

Who thought about giving their dog goat's milk? Apparently, someone did because it's part of the conversation these days. You may have already seen it in pet stores. Raw goat milk is often referred to as universal milk due to its easy digestibility for all mammals. It contains a variety of essential nutrients, including macro-minerals, micro-trace minerals, vitamins, protein, and more. In contrast to cow's milk, which undergoes commercial homogenization, goat's milk is naturally homogenized, which breaks down fat molecules into smaller sizes that are easier for digestion. Additionally, the body can absorb the micronutrients present in goat's milk much more efficiently than those in cow's milk (Holistic Hound, 2016). It's also less acidic than cow's milk. If you have a puppy, goat's milk is fine to have on the menu. Otherwise, while it is okay to feed goat's milk to adult dogs, my preference is not to do so. Reason one is because it adds more fat on the menu. Reason two is because no animals (such as wild dogs) drink milk once they are grown. Unfortunately, humans do, but it is inflammatory and can cause cancer. It can also trigger food sensitivities in humans and pets. You will want to keep in mind that it can produce allergens and mucus.

Next, let's cover quinoa, millet, and amaranth. All three are whole-grain foods. However, they're not cereal grains. They're edible seeds and referred to as pseudo cereals because they share similar characteristics with whole-grain cereals.

Pseudo cereals are plants that bear fruits or seeds that are utilized and consumed like grains, despite the fact that they are not classified as true cereal grains or grasses. Pseudo cereals are known for their high protein and nutrient content, gluten-free nature, and categorization as whole grains (Rotkovitz, 2020). All of these are a few types of cooked foods that I suggest, and that's due to particular nutrients, protein levels, and amino acids. However, the cooking directions on heavy flaked desaponified quinoa are minimal to none. If you do use it, you're still able to stay raw. I use the raw version.

Quinoa is a grain-like crop, but it's not a real cereal or grain. It is a seed (Szalay, 2018). It's more like a vegetable and is related to species like spinach and beets. Sometimes called a superfood, quinoa provides high-quality protein and other nutrients. Quinoa stands out among millets and amaranth because it is low in carbs, high in protein, and has all necessary amino acids. It is a complete protein source and contains all nine essential amino acids (Ask The Scientists, n.d.). Neither humans nor dogs can produce all of the essential amino acids on their own so we must get them from our food. Quinoa is also packed with several important nutrients, including magnesium, manganese, phosphorus and zinc.

Quinoa can be challenging. Some people love it and some people hate it. Dog owners who can't stand quinoa are ones who I've noticed buying cheaper brands that are not desaponified. On top of that, they're usually not rinsing or boiling it properly. You know it's not being done correctly if you see undigested quinoa in your dog's poop. Even when my dog had poor digestion, I never saw quinoa in his feces. If you do see that, you want to mash the food more. It's obvious your dog's digestive tract is still healing if you're sure you've boiled or steamed the quinoa enough. Remember, it should be translucent. On another note, what you're mashing, cooking and feeding is relative to your dog's current digestive state and how far along you are in the cycle between moving from pet feed to pet food. It all varies on the health of your dog's digestive tract. Mashing in any form helps with digestion and preventing blockages in gulpers. Again, I would opt for the flaked.

Before folks completely give up on it, I recommend trying the desaponified quinoa flakes. I saw huge gains in my dog's muscle structure when I started using it. It helps him feel fuller longer. (Saponin is a chemical compound and natural detergent naturally found in some plants, like quinoa. Desaponified quinoa means that the saponin is removed, which enables it to retain the full nutrient profile and makes it more bioavailable. When quinoa is desaponified, it's not an antinutrient. Antinutrients are compounds that interfere with how a body absorbs and utilizes nutrients. Common antinutrients include lectins, phytic acid, oxalic acid, tannins, and more.)

Quinoa is an item where you get what you pay for. I recommend purchasing a high quality organic desaponified quinoa. It's highly digestible. My favorite style is organic shredded, which is also called organic flakes.

I use quinoa three days a week on veggie and fruit days. Do not use quinoa on meat days or fast days. You can feed quinoa cooked or uncooked. (This is the only food in the book where cooking is alright, if you must.) Flaked is best. Then, I mix the quinoa into his food. My dog loves the sticky texture and consistency. Every dog likes them differently, so experiment with the texture. Some dogs may like smooshy quinoa while other dogs prefer it more formed.

Millets are a diverse group of small-seeded grasses grown globally as grains or cereal crops for animal feed and human consumption (Wikipedia, n.d.). Unlike quinoa, millets are higher in carbohydrates and have less protein. One benefit of adding millets on your dog's menu is that it is exceptionally cheap, but for me, it does not beat quinoa.

Amaranth is known as an ancient grain. This highly adaptable and healthy grain is rich in protein, fiber, micronutrients, and antioxidants, and it is naturally gluten-free. Specifically, amaranth provides a notable amount of manganese, magnesium, phosphorus, and iron (Link, 2018). Also, amaranth has a bit more protein than quinoa does (Bob's Red Mill, 2018).

I have never heard or read of dogs having bad experiences with quinoa, millets, or amaranth. As usual, you want to see if your dog will eat each of these foods. Take note of his preferences. My little guy does enjoy the former and latter.

To summarize, pay attention to the foods your dog enjoys. Notice which ones your dog gravitates toward, and which ones are shunned. Make a list or mental note and move forward accordingly.

Are Any Grains Good for Your Dog? The Controversy Dispelled

First of all, dogs do not need grains. Grains do not fulfill a nutritional need. If your dog eats grain, some here and there, she will probably not experience any problems. However, grains should not be a recurring mainstay on your dog's menu. Oats, rice, and wheat can cause digestive issues for some dogs over short windows of time. Feeding a dog grain for months on end can, over the long term, cause arthritis and create problematic skin issues.

In the past, it was commonly thought that wolves and wild dogs consumed grains by way of the stomach contents of their fresh prey. The research shed light on this thought and revealed that they avoid the contents of the stomach. They go straight for the internal organs. In other words, they go for the meat (Mech, 2007).

In recent years, we have seen domesticated dogs more than happy to eat grains in commercial dog feed. This may cause someone to question why dogs would avoid grains. However, the problem is that the grains are intentionally and heavily disguised. In other words, the pet industry psychologically tricks your dog into eating grains by the rich alluring scent of meat in the dog feed. Dogs literally think they are eating meat when they're not. This is likely because the grains were cooked in meat stock.

Regarding whether your dog wants grains, I don't need a reference for this. Pour some grains into your dog's bowl and see what happens. He or she will look up at you with a face that says, "What is this? Surely you don't think I'm going to eat this, right?" You've seen that look before, I'll bet.

What's the Real Truth About Oils and Balancing Diets with Fat?

Never feed your dog oils. Wolves and wild dogs never had oils out in nature throughout the entire lifespan of their species. There is no credible scientific evidence I have ever seen advocating for dogs to digest oils in relation to their specific nutritional needs. Both nature and science indicate that it's best to not feed your dog oils.

The only related argument I've read about this is that someone may complain their malnourished or underfed dog has bad skin. The skin may be flaking or severely dry, which would be obvious. In this circumstance, someone may put oil on their dog's skin to remedy it. However, it only remedies a symptom. The goal, as you have read about several times, is to implement an inside-out approach to health. Want to clean up a dog's skin? The solution is to clean up his diet, and it's the same for people too.

What about balancing fats? Examples of these include, but are not limited to, oils like coconut, fish, flax, and hemp. There is talk among raw feeders that you need to balance fats. This came about because animals bred for consumption have a higher level of omega-6 fats in comparison to omega-3 fats, when compared to their species living in the wild.

Numerous blogs say this difference in those two fats leads to chronic inflammation (Gunnars, 2018). I'm sure you can guess what happened next. To balance out the fats, raw feeders began adding omega-3 to their dog's foods. Mostly, they used coconut, fish, hemp, and flax seed oils. However, their efforts to balance the fats with "correct" ratios fall flat. Packing oils into your dog's menu will not prevent or reduce inflammation, nor will it improve her overall health. Plus, depending on how flax, for instance, is given, it can be rancid. If you're feeding flax and you grind it, make sure you place it in water for 15 minutes prior to feeding so it is rehydrated. It's best not to feed it dry.

Can your dog eat raw fish? Yes. That's totally fine. If your dog is healthy with a good immune system, parasites are not a problem (Scott, 2020). However, you want to ensure the fish comes from a quality source. As you probably know, fish have both omega-6 and omega-3. Oily fish is considered the most excellent source of omega-3s, while plant oils, nuts, and seeds contain omega-6s and omega-9s (Robertson, 2020).

What about inflammation? My take is the primary factor that creates inflammation in your dog is his fat consumption. I'm not saying it's bad for a dog to consume any or a small amount of fat. I am saying too much fat can prompt inflammation to get a foothold on your dog. This applies to both chronic and acute inflammation. The onset of acute inflammation is rapid and typically subsides within two weeks. On the other hand, chronic inflammation is a slower and typically milder type of inflammation that occurs when the body is unable to eliminate harmful substances or repair an injury, resulting in a prolonged state of inflammation that can persist for months or even years (CBSH Health, 2020).

This inflammation, which can result in early cell death and the growth of cancer cells, is a common underlying cause of chronic diseases such as cancer, heart disease, diabetes, digestive disorders, autoimmune disease, and Alzheimer's (Shagoury, 2017). To effectively treat diseases, healthcare providers must address the root cause of inflammation by creating a healthy environment that supports cellular health and function. This can involve lifestyle changes, such as a healthy diet, stress reduction, sufficient sleep, and regular exercise, as well as eliminating environmental factors like toxins and pollutants that contribute to inflammation and disease. Autoimmune diseases, which create inflammatory conditions that open the gates for other diseases and lead to death, are the number-one killer of humans and dogs in the U.S. (US National Library of Medicine National Institutes of Health, 2000).

If you find yourself worried about inflammation in your dog, keep the inside-out approach in mind. Aim at reducing her fat consumption instead of adding omega-3s or any other fats. Also, keep in mind that you can lower the omega-6 fats your dog is eating by cutting fat off meats and by putting more lean meats on the menu.

One topic related to oils is essential oils. Although not an oil for consumption, essential oils have gained in popularity through the years. Numerous essential oils are outright poisonous to animals, including eucalyptus, tea tree, cinnamon, lemon, peppermint, pine, wintergreen, and ylang-ylang. These are harmful whether they are licked up after an accident, used in diffusers, or applied to the skin. It's essential to remember that compared to people, animals like cats and dogs are much more sensitive to smells. What you might consider to be a small, pleasant fragrance could be overpowering and harmful to an animal (Cabbagetown Pet Clinic, 2020). If you use essential oils for yourself or your family, be sure to keep them out of reach of your pets. I use them infrequently in my diffuser from time to time. I also only use top-grade organic as I don't want to breathe toxic chemicals with my oil. The only oil I have found that gives my doggie "zen" is a bit of Frankincense straight or a little lavender straight. If my boy has issues with any scents, I get sneezes from him. That makes it obvious what he can and cannot take.

What Do I Do If My Dog Eats Anything and Everything?

If you have a teenage child, you probably know what it's like to have a body in your house that eats anything and everything! Sometimes dogs can have that "eat everything in sight" mentality too.

If your dog is a gorger or a gulper, here's what you need to know: It's not your fault. Some dogs are simply gulpers. With lots of patience and positive reinforcement, a dog can be taught to slow down. I had to do it with mine. I also had to find tricks, like packing a small bowl with his portion of meat, so he licks to eat it versus gulps. It works well. This helped him learn that his belly and digestion felt way better afterward. It's in a dog's nature for whatever reason. It likely relates to their ancestral pack days from long ago or how they were with their littermates.

Concerning gorging, "After catching and killing their food, wolves may eat up to 20% of their body weight. That is like eating 80 quarter-pound hamburgers at one sitting! Wolves in the wild may not get to eat every day and must gorge when they get the chance" (Wolf Park, n.d.). Since wolves did not eat daily, they were able to eat 20% of their body weight. Their food intake had to last up to 12 days, although that would fluctuate depending on prey being available. Although the math is not a precise science (yet), the feeding percentages you'll learn later in the book relate to what we know about wolves.

This means they eat food, and, quite often, they eat inedible objects as well. You know what I'm talking about if you've ever had to buy your roommate new shoes because your dog chowed down on them, or if your dog vacuums lint like mine used to do occasionally. With dogs like this, it's important for you to call the shots. Work to give him foods that have been present in the wild ... the food of his ancestors, wolves, and wild dogs, so he learns to only eat foods, not inedible objects. I had to spend time talking mine out of eating things from the yard, and eventually, with patient consistency, they understand; plus, feeding them before they go out helps. Most challenges can be thought through to a quick fix, which is better and more comfortable for you both, no matter what it might be, and if you get stumped, those items make for great consultations.

We have talked about feeding your dog unprocessed and natural foods, focusing on foods he enjoys and wants. As you focus on what they are eating, you're on poop patrol! Check out the history of her poop. Are there any foods in there that you recognize? (Color does not count, FYI.) If so, the body chose not to use it or was not able to use that specific food. In its wisdom, the body elected to eliminate the food rather than process it; some of this can change as their digestion heals. It truly depends on whether they are just starting on the diet or if you are beyond six months to a year, and how many medications they may have been on. These are all variables to keep in mind. Keep a running list of these types of foods for reference. Eliminate them from your menu for your dog as you learn about each one.

From there, replace those foods with other foods. You want to focus on giving your dog food that her body readily accepts and easily digests.

Just so you know the full story, it's possible that the undigested food is there for different reasons. This could include overeating or certain stress the body was experiencing at the time. For example, when you're moving to a new house, it's usually stressful for most dogs.

It's safe to say it could also be the emotions your dog is dealing with, so you may want to try foods a couple of times before opting them out if your dog enjoys them, or smash them or blend them if it's a situation where their digestive tract is still healing and they are not breaking down many items; if that works, then great. A good way to tell if their digestive tract is healing is seeing mucus in the poop or seeing the poop look browner overall.

CHAPTER 8

Species Appropriate Diet Examples and Guidelines

CONGRATS! You have now arrived at what I call the "meat" of this book. I'm going to lay out the Species Appropriate Feeding in detail for you. I'll explain the areas included first, and then I will get into the specific details.

Species Appropriate Feeding Options

What makes this nutrition plan different is that you feed your dog single kinds of food rotated on different days. The goal is to make sure the two main types of foods—meats and plants—do not touch or combine inside of your dog's single-chamber stomach. This way of feeding removes the toxic burden. In doing so, your dog's body may heal from its current disease state, allergy, etc., and stay healthy. This depends on your dog's current stage of life. The discussion of fat on meats and synthetic supplements also has come into play throughout this book to explain the overall toxic burden on the body. This will also be discussed in more depth so you have a clear understanding of how this diet can optimize your dog's life.

As you read earlier, you are welcome to combine all different sorts of plant foods in a single meal. My dog has never had issues implementing that technique. You can feed your dog the same dish every plant day if you want. You're also welcome to have a separate day for fruits and a separate day for veggies if you prefer. We often do that, as my dog is really not into combining foods. I can barely ever get away with that with him.

You can also mix in fasting days. This is where you get to be flexible and creative, paying special attention to how your dog responds. You're a strong informed owner now! Within this framework, you can customize your nutrition plan based on your dog's likes and dislikes and as you see fit.

Moving forward, I will cover basic instructions. Following that section, I will cover what I call alternative strategies. There, you can customize your plan further, if need be, based on your dog's condition, age, personality, and so on. Keep in mind you're not picking one customized plan within the Species Appropriate Feeding framework and sticking rigidly to it forever. I give starting points and options. You can vary them based on your new relationship with your dog and what you're observing. With knowledge comes responsibility. The beauty of this knowledge is that it increases health and wellness for your pet.

Within this framework, you can change it, build on it, and adapt it as you go and as your dog's needs and preferences shift. It is the flexibility of this diet that makes it so enjoyable, both for you and your dog. If you only have certain foods in the house that day or ones that your doggie chooses, like mine, vegetables instead of fruits that day will work fine. Certain dogs are easier going than others, as you know. My dog has a much more demanding palate on certain days. So much so, that I ask him what he wants. He has truly determined the menu and sequence over the years.

Guidelines for Fasting Day

A fasting day entails only serving fresh filtered water. Preferably, you would fast your dog for 24 hours. It is thought that this 24-hour period gives your dog's stomach the margin to digest and clear out the meat day items. This ensures meats and plants do not touch. It's also a nice, short detox and gives your dog's digestive system a reprieve to start healing. Although I do recommend this, it is optional. Some dogs' systems eliminate the waste content around the 20-hour mark, and that could be relative to many factors based on their age and the health of their digestive system. Remember, you know your dog's health concerns and personality. Apply the knowledge of this book as you see fit. If you do not want to have a transitional fasting day, the next best option is to begin with a plant day feeding as I mentioned above.

If you have a gorger or gulper who eats anything and everything, watch him closely on fasting day! You will probably need to carefully supervise your dog to the extent possible. Ensure only fresh water enters her system and not inedible things in the yard or while on a walk. Block off access to any trash and anything else that commonly tempts your dog. Restrict access to anything that is not healthy or is poisonous for dogs. Other items to consider hiding or safeguarding could range from socks and old, decaying toys to used tissue paper. This list includes stuff you may not ordinarily think of that your dog usually does not go after. As your dog heals, her energy and enthusiasm will increase pretty quickly.

Although your dog may not be happy with you on fasting day and may not understand it (especially if you have never done it), remember that it is for his own good. They do adjust. We embrace our fasting day together nowadays. It happily lands on Sundays. Every Sunday, we sleep in too. With this framework, you can build convenient flexibility so you can enjoy it as much as we do. Fasting is healthy and helpful for your dog's body. Give yourself the personal freedom to not feel guilty. My boy rests up more and sleeps, not having to worry about eating. As you now may be able to see, it's all in how you approach it, just like anything in life.

Guidelines for Meat Day

Let's talk about the most exciting day for your dog, the day he may show you a little extra affection and love … you guessed it: meat day! We love our meat days. I prepare them two to three days per week, and he fasts on the third or fourth day, giving me a break while he enjoys all his favorite meats. So, it's three- or four-days total: meat, meat, fast or meat, meat, meat, fast. We make our meat days extra special, and we do have more fun shenanigans. And yes, you better believe that I get woken up early that day. It doesn't bother me one bit! His energy and enthusiasm are phenomenal, and even though I am not a real morning person, I am to see his beautiful face staring at me to get up or the massive nub wiggling. That's what you can expect from your happy, energetic dog too.

TIP 6

Two options for feeding on meat day:

1. Feed your dog meat for one meal on meat day.

2. Divide up the meat into two different meals on meat day.

You can experiment with both methods to see which one your dog responds best to and prefers. Feeding times: This is your call. It comes down to what works best for you and your schedule.

Meat Temperature

Feed your dog meats at room temperature or slightly warmer to see how he responds. Meats can be left out for 24 hours or more prior to feeding, whether it's fresh or frozen. My boy prefers all his meats cooler with that fresh feel. Again, it's not a perfect science. It is my dog's preference.

Puppies

Feeding a puppy? If so, it's usually best to avoid feeding that cute loving ball of energy late at night. Feed her more frequently throughout the day than you would an adult dog. My little guy actually did require a full tummy to sleep through the night. Again, it's the puppy's choice on this one. Experiment and see what works best!

Meat Day Bone Option

You can add in a "just for fun" bone on meat day if you want. Give him neck bones from pork, venison, or beef. (Never use weight-bearing femur bones.) Pork obviously has more fat. Don't always do those on meat days. I do not use those. Remember, no femur bones. Those can break your dog's teeth and have no nutritional value (other than fat). My little guy chews like a 200-pound dog! Factor in how aggressive your dog is and how hard of a chewer your dog may be, so he does not end up with a cracked tooth at worst or tooth pain at best. We never want our dogs in pain.

Types of Meat

You can use a single meat or different types. Be creative. See what your dog prefers. There is no need to rotate different meats. It's all protein. I do liver, heart, and kidney with beef and a little chicken and bone to finish our mix. You can make it as complex or as simple as you like. We go all-out on our meat days. Everything is organic, grass-fed, and grass finished where possible. I always use organic because we had some pretty major disease states to work through, as oftentimes organic has the highest nutrient content and lowest amount of chemicals theoretically. The more you learn and understand how food is created and raised, the more you'll learn that it really depends on the specific farms and farmers, whether it's organic or not. I was critical of everything that went on my dog and in his body for the first year and beyond until I saw most items resolved. Eventually, as a body heals, it will be able to overcome everyday toxins and detox as bodies are designed to do. You have to restore your pet before allowing them to experience toxins in everyday life.

Meat-to-Bone Ratio

There is no need to do the math for this. Instead, observe her poop. Implement enough bone to keep her poop solid following a meat day. Make sure it's solid and looks healthy. If you do not include bone, certain necessary nutrients will be missing. I am sure you have noted from previous chapters that loose poops will happen for some dogs. If you have loose poop on meat days, add more bone. Keep adding bone until you reach the proper consistency.

Treats

You can make treats from what's known as secreting organs (called offal), such as kidneys, livers, and spleens. Another option is to add those organs to a meat day meal two to four times per month. The organs responsible for producing and releasing substances in an animal's body are packed with essential nutrients and perform critical biological roles for survival. On the other hand, meat and bone may not contain all the necessary nutrients, making it essential to incorporate raw liver and other organs into a diet for optimal health (LeJeune, n.d.).

What do you do if your dog refuses to eat the raw meat? Patience is the key to success when you are making the transition. Be calm and understanding (Marshall, n.d.). Make it a positive and fun experience. After all, our dogs take cues from us that you may not even notice. Just be neutral, ask what they think and make an offering. They are amazing beings who observe everything we do. No pressure, right?

Let me share a tip that worked for me when I first started feeding my dog raw meals. Once you've put the food in front of your dog, don't hover but try to step back and let them enjoy it. If you have a really eager and participative dog like mine, you might want to stick around for the first few times. I remember when I gave my dog his first raw chicken leg, he looked at me with excitement, like he was saying, "Is this for me?" And of course, it was! Seeing his happy face with the biggest smile let me know I had finally gotten it right. From then on, we tried many new foods and observed several health changes as we kept moving forward, and again, this also reinforced that I finally had it right. It was a great experience for both me and my furry friend!

After placing the uncooked food in front of your dog, leave and allow him to solve the problem of how to eat it. Wait for about 15 minutes. If your dog has not yet eaten the food, calmly remove it and try again at the next feeding interval. At that point, you may need to change the item. After all, dogs know what they like. In the beginning, there may be a little trial and error. It's totally fine to be flexible and come half way by giving it a second shot, or by switching up the raw item after a second try until you find the items your pet really loves. It's ok to have some trial and error. (Marshall, n.d.). My boy is very specific. He yells and bounces around for his food. Although it rarely happens, if I do not give the correct item, he looks at it like it is poison and walks away. Given that I have closely observed him, this immediately lets me know how he feels. After that, I'd go with the next item he would have in his sequence and it's always worked. Dogs get tired of the same stuff at times and how much depends on the dog.

Make sure you don't inject any negativity into anything related to food. For example, if you only eat fruit and happen to think meat is gross, your dog will pick up on that. We must be fair to our carnivorous bouncing bundles of joy.

All dogs are different. You want to check to make sure you are not feeding items they have not chosen. It's also possible they aren't hungry or are detoxing. Sometimes my little guy isn't hungry. I always say, "It's okay. We can eat it later." This way, he feels it is okay to eat only when he is hungry. He knows he does not have to eat to make me happy. In the past, I used to beg him to eat food. I would hand-feed him, thinking he was picky. When you feed a dog properly, they aren't picky. At least, my boy is no longer picky. I can tell you that my boy has never refused raw meat since his first-ever raw chicken leg.

Here's another helpful tip. If raw meat is not enticing to your dog, try braising it in a frying pan. Make sure that he watches you do this. They'll equate the action with food. It may help them make the connection.

Meats served to your dog must be raw and come from a reputable source. Here's the list of recommended raw meats that your dog can eat (in no particular order): lean beef, lamb, pork, rabbit, venison, buffalo, Cornish game hen, quail, fish, offal, green tripe, and chicken (whole, carcass, or frame).

I always use organic meats, and I order from two private farms online. I looked into commercialized organic meat at the supermarket, and I was not pleased.

Meats List Details

Here are helpful insights about certain meats found on the list.

- Offal: This may be something you haven't heard of before. Sometimes offal is referred to as variety meat. Different types of offal are "any of various non-muscular parts of the carcasses of beef and veal, mutton and lamb, and pork, which are either consumed directly as food or used in the production of other foods" (Encyclopedia Britannica, n.d.). These include liver from chicken, pork, and beef, beef kidney and heart, and chicken giblets which consist of liver, heart, and gizzards (Dog Nutrition Naturally, n.d.). Offal simply includes internal parts like tissues and organs along with external parts such as hide and horns. It's no surprise that some of these are usually not for human consumption. However, I eat liver, heart, and kidney frequently when my dog does. In fact, I eat most of his diet so we can share ... all but the raw meat of course!
  - ✦ Liver and kidney: Feed these to your dog less frequently, as they are rich. Cut fat off these items.
  - ✦ Tongue, brains, heart, giblets, and the like can be fed to your dog on a regular basis, and heart as much as you like. Simply be mindful of his overall fat intake and, of course, cut fat off these items.
- Green tripe: Although it may not make your mouth water, this meat, which refers to unbleached and unprocessed stomach lining of either lamb or beef, is considered a highly nutritious superfood for dogs (K9Natural, n.d.). Serve it raw. Raw tripe

that is green is crucial for your dog's diet as cooking can eliminate digestive enzymes (Scott, 2019). Green tripe also contains partially digested greens, which is healthy for your dog. It's best to confirm the cows were grass-fed up to the point of death because sometimes they're fed grains toward their final days. Always check the labels to confirm. An animal's final meals determine what goes into your dog's body.

- Quail, Cornish game hens, and rabbit: Your dog can eat the entirety of these animals. Simply trim off any fat and skin.
- Buffalo and beef: Eye of round is typically the least fatty. Try to get the least fatty items, and always cut the fat out. Some folks choose not to feed beef to their dog, as it can take work if you don't get the least fatty cuts. Overall, bison is pretty fat-free. Remember to never select ground meats, as you don't know how much fat is ground in them. If it's anything but straight red meat, there's fat in it.
- Muscle meat: Feeding your dog only muscle meat can potentially lead to diarrhea. This is a fairly common occurrence. If it happens, don't be surprised. The solution is to add meat that has edible bones like turkey, chicken, game hen, etc., as mentioned earlier.
- Reminder: Never grind raw meat unless there is a real need. If you do, always work toward not grinding if you can. There are rare circumstances of dogs without teeth and those with major digestive issues who were on lots of medications, typically. In those cases, while digestive tracts are healing, or if they are massively gulping or vomiting up food, I grind raw bones for nutrient absorption. This way, the dog gets the nutrients necessary from bones. You can also grind some and teach your dog how to safely chew a bone each time until you're comfortable.

Grinding is a way to ease into it so you're not as stressed (especially if you have been scared of bones). Remember, raw bones are fine. It's the cooked bones that splinter and create shards. I did grind bones for my dog initially, as he was horribly sick. I had major stress and wanted to make sure that if he got sick, it wasn't from what I was doing. He was a gulper too. Rather than leave him nutritionally deficient by not including bone, I ground it up nice and fresh. It was truly like a delicacy to him.

- Whole chickens: Dogs usually love whole chickens, game hens, and quail. Chewing larger bones of a chicken can be difficult if you have a smaller dog. In that case, the quail, chicken wings, or Cornish hens above are a better choice. Remember to trim the fat and remove skin. As you may recall, fat is where the toxins are stored in our bodies, both in farm-raised animals and our pets.
- Chicken carcasses and chicken frames: While these do give your dog the softest and smallest bones to chew, they obviously do not have much flesh for your dog to enjoy. Therefore, it's best to add more meat when serving these. Trim off any fat before serving.
- Fish: This option for meat comes down to what your dog will prefer. If you live near water, it could be an outstanding option. You already know purchasing fish can get expensive. Cheaper options are sardines, smelt, and even fish heads. The smaller fish tend to have less metal issues, such as mercury. Work to find a solid, reputable distributor. I prefer ones who freeze them right in the boat. Humans need to worry about fish bones, but dogs do not.
- Eggs: Although not a meat, check to see whether your dog will eat eggs. You can serve them with or without the shell. Eggs are great because they're easy to find and cheap. Many experts

advise not to feed eggs to dogs more than one or two times per week. The other consideration is that you must be mindful that eggs are adding fat to your dog's diet. I personally don't feed them, as my dog is not lacking any nutrients because he's on the species appropriate feeding plan.

Guidelines for Fruit Day

Fruits can be a bit confusing because dog owners wonder about how often, how much, whether to mix one fruit with others, and so on. How about we keep it simple?

First

Serving your dog fruits is a legitimate meal. It's not a snack. You are welcome to mix in or add veggies or greens if you choose. I serve straight fruits on fruit day given there are so many choices, and it's in line with feeding a particular category of food per day. If you feed greens mixed in with your fruits, these are some good choices: spinach, collard, beet, turnip, kale, spinach. I generally feed three items of fruit per meal.

Second

Fruits are known for their healing properties. That is why it's very common for dogs or clients who are recovering from procedures to be served fruits. Numerous food options, such as fruits, vegetables, healthy plant-based fats, and sources of protein, have been proven to decrease inflammation, boost the immune system, aid in the healing process, and supply the necessary energy for recovery. (Kubala, 2020). Fruits assist in improving skin and hair, along with boosting the immune system (Dreher, 2018) (Romero, 2012). Another bonus is that fruits are easy for a body to digest. This goes for both canines and people.

Third

You get to decide whether you want to do a fruit-only day or a vegetable-only day. The other option is doing one day with both fruits and vegetables. For example, this could include butternut squash and quinoa with red peppers. That meal is very popular with my boy. At times, you may need to look up some items to be sure you have them on the right days. I know I did at first.

How to feed fruits to your dog:

- Serve immediately, serve pre-prepared thawed, or serve refrigerated fruit when it's a little warmer.
- Serve different fruits together if you want. (Do not blend them together.)
- Fresh fruit is ideal. It's best to avoid frozen fruits. However, many dogs enjoy frozen blueberries as opposed to fresh. I know mine does. If you do that, it isn't uncommon for the smaller dogs to shake after eating them, as they get cold.
- Serving room-temperature fruits is best, like with anything. It's not the best idea to pull out fruits from your fridge and dump them in his or her bowl. In the summer, it may be more welcome. Just observe your dog and see what they like.
- Use a knife to cut up the fruits. Make them bite-size for whatever is in line with your type and size of dog. Bigger bites for larger dogs. Smaller bites for smaller dogs. Sometimes for longer items like zucchini, I cut them the long way to make it like a bone. If you have a gulper, cut them small to avoid

choking. Do this while you're teaching your dog to patiently slow down and enjoy her food. The more they chew and engage their parasympathetic system, the more nutrients are assimilated and absorbed, just like in humans.
- Serve with veggies if you want. This can cause gas sometimes, so watch out for that and, if so, don't combine them. Plus, certain vegetables are gassier than others. It's just as uncomfortable and sometimes painful for them as it is for us.
- You can serve one, two, or three fruit meals on a fruit day.
- Do not show emotions when serving your dog food. Do not act nervous or worried. Do not disguise the food. Refuse to coax your dog. Do not get emotionally attached to him eating. Present the food very matter-of-factly, without emotion, or in a positive and enjoyable way. This allows the dog to choose what they like without any queues from you. As you know, your queues can turn them on to food, or away from food that they would otherwise enjoy.
- Most dogs enjoy bananas, figs, apples, pears, persimmons, ripe berries (as the seasons allow), and even melons.
- Melons: See whether your dog enjoys having the rind or not.
- It comes down to your dog's preferences. Since some dogs throw them up, I skip them. Always feed all melons a few hours away from other fruit. This way, they go through the system super quick. It's best they don't run into the veggies because the combination can create diarrhea. They tend to be purged quickly by the system due to the fruit alcohols created. This can also create fermentation, which leads to gas. The reason is that the previous food is slower moving and leads to cellular degradation. Also, melons digest so quickly and flush the system due to the high-water content. Again, this can cause

fermenting, which creates gas or diarrhea. The system can go into a detox flush, essentially purging everything, which can cause dehydration.

- You don't want melons running into other foods, especially meat. Now, in this context, this is just the case for melons. It's something to be aware of when feeding or combining plants. I give a full 24 hours after every meat meal before feeding fruits or any foods. As a rule of thumb, either meat, a 24-hour fast, then melon/fruit OR meat, a vegetable like butternut squash (or your dog's favorite squash) and quinoa mix, if feasible, the following day, then a fruit/melon day after that day. This keeps it on the safe side for digestion and helps avoid painful gas.
- Berries: As with all berries, feed your dog the entire berry as a whole. For strawberries, remove the stem. With apples, remove the core and the stem. More than likely, that's how you prepare those for yourself.
- Peeling: There's no need to peel pears or apples. You are welcome to see whether your dog prefers those fruits having peels or not. As usual, observe your dog's poop. If you see big pieces of fruit skins, it will be best for you to peel it after all.
- Grapes: Grapes are fine to serve. As with other fruits, some dogs will eat them and some will not.
- Dried fruits: I only recommend serving these in moderation. Fresh is the healthiest choice.
- If you notice any problems like poop that has fruit in it or vomiting, implement different fruits. You can also smash them if your dog likes them that way. Use one of those techniques until their digestive tract heals. If it continues to happen, change to other fruits. You can experiment to see which fruit

is the culprit. Once discovered, you can eliminate it from the menu if necessary.

Will my dog eat fruit after a day of fasting? You'll be pleased to know that most dogs will. If a dog does not, there's no need for alarm or worry. When dogs are hungry, they will eat fruits (or veggies). Remember, like wolves, their primary food of choice is meat (aka prey). Sometimes when a dog does not eat, it's simply a signal that she is not hungry. Sometimes a dog may not want to eat fruits and veggies, as he is full from eating meat the day before. When dogs eat secondary (supplemental) foods, it is usually because their stomachs are empty, and they are genuinely hungry. It's totally normal for your dog to eat less of whatever you're feeding after a fast day.

Guidelines for Vegetable Day

If you skipped ahead to this section, it's important for you to know that you get to decide whether you want to do a vegetables-only day and a fruits-only day on your feeding plan. The third option is doing one day with both fruits and vegetables. This would be called a mixed category plant day, but either way, you should know that a species appropriate diet does not really call for vegetables per se. Only occasionally in the wild will wolves come across veggies to eat. When they do, they can process those veggies in their raw forms. If you want a species appropriate diet, you would limit vegetables. I'm mentioning it below because I know people will feed them anyway.

How to serve your dog vegetables:

- Serve vegetables raw. Avoid cooking them to maintain a species appropriate diet and feed sparingly.

- You can either blend the veggies with a blender, cut them lengthwise, or finely chop them. These methods are the safest. Doing so helps avoid obstructions with dogs that gulp and dogs with poor digestion transitioning. Keep vegetables to a minimum as this helps you stay within a species appropriate diet.
- Some cruciferous vegetables may create gas in some dogs. The ones that produce the most gas are broccoli, cauliflower and Brussels sprouts. Monitor your dog after feeding. If he is fine, it's fine to continue serving those specific veggies.
- What about avocado? You can serve a little if you like. Remember to remove the pit and skin. Despite being a plant fat, it's still fat. That's why you should only serve a little.
- What about sweet potatoes? I tried sweet potatoes for a couple of weeks with my dog and it did not go well. He would either throw up because he would try to stuff himself, or it was too heavy on his stomach. He also got bloated and had gas. I do not recommend potatoes, sweet potatoes or yams (cooked or raw) for dogs.
- Reminder: Vegetables with high cellulose content need to be served in small quantities (or not at all if they affect your dog). These include celery, broccoli, cauliflower, peas, carrots, legumes, and asparagus.
- Serve raw veggies at room temperature or slightly cooler. I often found that when I was preparing my dog's food, if I did not let it get to room temperature or cooler, it would make him throw up. Some dogs are very sensitive to the temperature of their food.
- Feed one to two meals per day. As dogs age, oftentimes digestion can wane a little bit. If you're not interested in adding a digestive enzyme, it's sometimes better to feed smaller meals more often so they do not lose too much weight.

- You can mix any of these with other veggies or fruits. For example, some people do quinoa and blueberries. I keep vegetables straight as it's just the way my dog prefers it.
- Quinoa is a wonderful addition to add and mix with veggies. Plus, as you know, it's a high-protein and low-fat food with the entire complement of amino acids.

There are more points to bring out. Some dogs are not fans of cruciferous veggies like broccoli, greens, or cauliflower. My dog ate them raw when I used to serve them. However, they do create gas in some dogs. If that happens after serving them, remove those items from your feeding list. As usual, you need to test one veggie by itself at a time to see if your dog will or will not eat it.

Picky eater? There is not really such a thing anymore on this diet because dogs are so thrilled to finally eat real food, but if your dog snubs any of these veggies, take a matter-of-fact approach. Do not add condiments or disguise them in any way. You need to genuinely know what your dog prefers and will eat and feed them what they choose.

Especially in November, dog owners ask about canned pumpkin. You can feed this to your dog. Feed your dog canned pumpkin sparingly. Remember it's commercialized and processed, and it is coming from a factory, not from nature. Pumpkin and fresh butternut squash are a huge hit for my little guy! When you see the color difference from fresh to frozen or canned, you will easily notice the nutritional difference (even though most times, frozen foods are most nutritious as they are left on the vines the longest) (ABC Health & Wellbeing / By staff writers, 2017).

One word of caution is to avoid feeding meat every day or even close to every day. Also, avoid eliminating meat from the nutrition plan. Both are extremes. As the saying goes, moderation is always best!

Food Percentage Starting Points and Ideal Dog Weight Breakdown

As a responsible pet owner, it is crucial to closely monitor your dog's physical condition and adjust their diet accordingly. For instance, if your dog has successfully reduced inflammation and achieved their optimal weight by following a species-appropriate diet, that's great news. However, if you notice that your dog's weight is dropping below the recommended range and they appear lethargic or thin, you must take action. Be sure you're not using detoxing symptoms as a justification to avoid increasing their food intake or reducing their exercise routine a little until their weight returns to normal. While healing, a dog shouldn't be underweight. And if they weren't at their ideal weight before starting a species-appropriate diet, they should aim to reach it.

Here are great starting guidelines about how much food to feed your dog depending on his or her current or desired body weight. A variety of sources share these average starting points (Hofve, 2020) (Raw Fed Dogs, n.d.).

- Meat = Start with 3% of his ideal weight.

- Plants = Start with 5% of his ideal weight.

My dog is roughly 26 pounds. I want to feed him 5% of the ideal weight on plant day. To get that amount, I take .05 multiplied by his weight (26 pounds). That equals 1.3 pounds (20.80 ounces per day, once or split in half for twice a day). Do the same thing for meat per day, only using .03.

Following is a convenient breakdown of how many ounces and pounds to feed each day based on your dog's weight, and of course, shift the percentage up or down depending on if you're trying to maintain, increase, or decrease weight loss.

Ideal Weight (lbs.)	Meat Day (oz. / lbs.)	Plant Day (oz. / lbs.)
10	4.80 / .30	8 / .50
20	9.60 / .60	16 / 1
30	14.40 / .90	24 / 1.50
40	19.20 / 1.20	32 / 2
50	24 / 1.50	40 / 2.50
60	28.80 / 1.80	48 / 3
70	33.60 / 2.10	56 / 3.50
80	38.40 / 2.40	64 / 4
90	43.20 / 2.70	72 / 4.50
100	48 / 3	80 / 5
110	52.80 / 3.30	88 / 5.50
120	57.60 / 3.60	96 / 6
130	62.40 / 3.90	104 / 6.50
140	67.20 / 4.20	112 / 7
150	72 / 4.50	120 / 7.50

Choosing a protocol is easy, as you can't go wrong with any of them overall, but as you can see, some are more geared to age or level of toxicity buildup over the years. You may want to consider your schedule and how much time you have for doggie outings or if you can be comfortable adding a doggie door and how much prep time you have. The protocols are flexible, and you can adjust them to meet your schedule. What you pick today may not be what you pick three months from now, so observation, flexibility, patience, and a keen level of predictable intuition will develop with your canine and guide you to making the best decisions for your dog.

You're always free to switch it up as needs change, health improves, or goals change with weight, etc. You'll just want to note that plants digest quicker than meat, so we always want plants going in first, then meat, then fast to give enough time in between the last meal and the next fruit meal to avoid them meeting up in the digestive tract, creating upset and gas. As you can imagine, gas can be really painful for some dogs more than others, just like us. Mine gets almost incapacitated if it's excessive at all.

If you're uncomfortable with fasting, try the Feeding Example 1. If your dog was heavily medicated for skin allergies or vaccinated yearly for many years, or has any long-term toxicity load, then it will help your dog's body unload the toxicity in a more comfortable manner.

Older dogs do benefit from more plant days, so it's a good option to do Feeding Example 2 all the way down to Feeding Example 4, depending on how much weight may be needed to lose. If you're comfortable with fasting and your dog was raw fed and doesn't have any major health issues, then Feeding Example 2 to Feeding Example 3 are great choices.

If you have a puppy and it needs to gain weight, choose a higher meat day protocol; if the pup needs to lose weight, choose a gradual step-down toward more and more plant days until you reach your desired goal. This can be the same advice for any dog starting the protocol to lose weight.

Overall advice: meat adds weight, plants take it off more, plants reverse disease quicker (fruit being the quickest and most effective) and fasting allows the dog to heal from symptoms they are having as they are detoxing. When the body is not digesting, it can focus all its energy on healing.

Slow and steady wins the race, so step up or down based on what you're observing in weight, detox symptoms, and overall energy. The body chooses what it detoxes first, and it will have the last word, so patience is key. It takes years to build toxins to a rate that causes disease unless a dog or even a person is more overwhelmed with toxins than their body can remove. Add improper feeding to their body, and we have the creation of disease you learned about earlier.

TIP 7

When you start, it's a best practice to fast for 24 hours. Do a minimum of 18 to 20 hours if your dog is really struggling. I was surprised how well my boy did since he had never fasted before, and because he mad loves his snackies. The fast allows all the old foods to move out. Then, feed a meal of carrots. This will give your dog a bright stool. Carrots are wonderful for their fiber content and help push out anything hanging on in the digestive tract. You will know you can proceed with the new foods without fruit or anything else creating tummy trouble by running into the old foods.

If diarrhea or vomiting occurs, fast for 24 hours and then feed a simple meal of bananas or a little butternut squash before returning to the protocol you choose. Make sure to always provide plenty of clean filtered water, and if you feel they need a little longer to expel whatever irritant they are moving out of their body, that's fine as well. Blocking symptoms creates toxicity, so it's best to let the body eliminate them. If you need filter ideas, the ones I use are on my page at the beginning and end of this book.

FEEDING EXAMPLES: MATCHING THEM TO YOUR DOG AND YOUR SCHEDULE, AND POSSIBLE OUTCOMES

FEEDING EXAMPLE 1
1 Meat day for every 1 Plant day

- Easy planning, tracking, and peace of mind if you're worried about fasting days.
- I would suggest feeding sometime in the morning only. This allows about 23 hours before the next feeding.

Suggested for
- Active adult dogs and younger dogs.

Daily Schedule
- Meat, Plant, Repeat.
- Number of Feedings: 1
- This diet does not have an official fast of 24 hours or more.

Cautions
- This creates higher fat consumption, which can be too high for some dogs.
- Make sure to remove all trimmable fat and skin.
- Watch stools to make sure they are compact and solid so you know if you're giving enough bone.

FEEDING EXAMPLE 2

2 Plant days for every 1 Meat day

Suggested for

- Can assist in weight and fat loss in dogs.
- Wonderful nutrition plan for older canines.
- Simple plan for dog owners to follow.

Daily Schedule

- Plant, Plant, Meat, Fast 24 hours, Repeat.
- Number of Feedings: 1-2

Cautions

- This plan does create weight loss and fat loss.

FEEDING EXAMPLE 3

1 Plant day to 2 Meat days (back to back) to 1 Fasting day

Suggested for

- Fasting day (every fourth day) gives the body a reprieve and digestive reset.
- Having meat days next to each other makes it easier for you to

keep the meat fresh.

Daily Schedule

- Plant, Meat, Meat, Fast 24 hours, Repeat.
- Number of Feedings: 1–2

Cautions

- If your dog is consuming too much fat, this will usually show up in the form of symptoms such as itchy skin or itchy ears. If your dog has these symptoms, lower the amount of meat served.

FEEDING EXAMPLE 4

3 Veggie days to every 1 Meat day

Suggested for

- There's flexibility on this plan, as you can extend it with 4 or 5 Veggie days in a row if you want.
- This keeps your dog on his toes and a bit in suspense as there can be a lot of variety.

Daily Schedule

- Veggie, Veggie, Veggie, Meat, Repeat.
- Number of Feedings: 1–2

Cautions

- This demands a bit more of you since you need to plan, prep, and prepare the veggies.

Recipe Samples and Bone Details

These are the items I use for my own dog that he has chosen for himself. He enjoys these the most. I have balanced the meals to make sure he gets all of the appropriate nutrient proportions. On meat days, we follow 80% muscle meat (which can include heart), 10% bone, and 10% internal organs (5% of that 10% being a type of liver). This breakdown comes from what I do based on my experience and what I have learned from my certifications on complete diets and feeding a species appropriate diet for your pet. Feel free to pair different food choices based on what your pet enjoys, with the categories above.

- My boy's meat days: Beef and chicken, internal organs such as hearts, liver, kidney, and corresponding bones for those items. I do vary these items. For example, sometimes beef liver, other times chicken liver and the same items for the rest of the internal organs.
- My boy's plant days: Butternut squash, red peppers, flaked raw quinoa mixed with water, and sprouted flax seeds (rehydrated in water for 15 minutes), blueberries or bananas. It also includes a teaspoon of sprouted pumpkin seed butter doggy lick that I make special, that my boy loves. Feel free to try mine first or see what your dog likes. Many owners have typically been experimenting and know what their dogs like, and that's fine too.

- Treat options for training: Some form of dehydrated beef liver or any other meat or internal organ that your pup or dog likes. Of course, you can dehydrate any plant snacks for plant days or any fruits for fruit days. Just keep meat treats on meat days, plant treats on plant days, and fruit treats on fruit days. There are no treats on fast days, just plenty of fresh filtered water. I make sure all of my water dishes are extra clean and full on those days. My trick is if I don't have time to make snacks, I just give 3-5 oz. (as my boy is 24 lbs.) of whatever we had for breakfast or a portion of it, if he needs a snack or if I have a meeting. If it's earlier I give the 5 oz., later the 3 oz., so I don't compromise his dinner too much. We just work it out and are super flexible, and honestly the more you pay attention, everything gets easier and quicker, and you find obvious ways to manage a hungry pup and not feel guilty if you can't pull away at that moment as you will be in a meeting. I give a snack if he needs one. It just works out.
- Bone details: One-third to one-fourth of the mixture is meat or internal organs, with the bone contained in it. Any extra space is added bone. You'll know you have enough bone when you can see poops turn white as they dry in the yard. My boy is a gulper, so even though I trained him to eat bones nicely, I still grind most, as it just gives me peace of mind, and he is older, so it's hard to teach an older dog to change something like that, so we work around it.

CHAPTER 9

Dog Chew Choices and Making Your Own Training Treats

A SPECIES APPROPRIATE DIET will clean up and optimize your dog's system by detoxifying it, realigning their gut and healing their digestive tract. This means you do not want to add junk, chemicals, or toxins by accident by using unhealthy chews or training treats. Everything you feed your dog matters. It all counts. Nothing is neutral, which is the same for humans when it comes to creating disease patterns. What you put in and on your pet matters daily, and that's a wonderful way to show your love and appreciation for all they give to you daily.

Concerning chews and training treats, I have obviously not tested everything on the market. As such, I always recommend using caution and doing your research. This goes for anything you're considering allowing your dog to consume. For the most part, dog owners give their dogs treats and chews with little to no strategy or thoughtfulness. Let me give you some guidelines and share my personal experiences.

Commercial chews are very popular. They're also usually very problematic. As with the pet feed industry, the goal is profit. Sometimes, there is a lack of transparency. Bottom line, if you don't make it, you don't truly know what's in it. That's just how it is. Most of the chews that adorn the shelves nowadays are chemically treated chews. As usual, the chemicals are on them to do something that is unnatural, like to preserve it. This could be anything from making chews have a long shelf life to modifying the shape, texture, or taste. Rawhide chews for pets can contain harmful substances and/or toxic chemicals in small amounts, similar to the way some pet toys may also contain them (Fetch by WebMD, n.d.). So, whether it's a chew toy or treat, the very best thing is for you to make them so you know what's in them. For example, let's say you order a doggie toy online and it has a squeaker inside. Everything is organic, except for the squeaker. Even if the company is following safety guidelines and using organic materials, since the squeaker is not organic, it's truly not a 100% organic product. Oftentimes, commercially-made products this way will claim their products are organic when they're not, while smaller businesses will be transparent and tell you the full truth. When companies make claims about their products, it can be wise to research. Find out whether or not you can safely trust the company with your dog's health. This goes for all products, toys and chews. As you can probably guess, I am super critical of anything that goes into or on my dog in any way because it really makes a difference year over year.

Let's start with the most popular chews, rawhides. Rawhide chews made in countries outside of the US are often treated with chemicals to preserve the product during transportation, meaning that when these chews are imported, they likely have higher levels of chemicals (Stebbins, 2019).

Here are some more natural popular treats followed by information about them:

- Hooves: While cheaper than antlers, these smelly treats can possibly cause digestive issues in dogs and crack their teeth. They did for my dog. They are really hard. They're also nice and stinky, so dogs love them. If you can find more malleable ones, they may be okay. The hard ones were too hard for my boy because he chews as if he believes he weighs 200 pounds. If you also have that type of chewer in a 24-pound dog, I'd find something more reasonable. If you want to feed hooves, try horse hooves. When farriers trim horse feet, they often give the trimmings to dogs and the dogs love them!

- Antlers: If they are not treated with dyes or synthetic chemicals, they are most likely safe. Although they can cost more, the price tag of antlers can vary depending on the size, type, and quality. If your dog has dental issues, you can purchase ground antlers or make your own at home. You can also get the half cut antlers that expose the marrow and make them more malleable. Ground antler is a super choice if you happen to not have ground bone pulled out for a short-term solution on a meat day.

- Pig ears: These treats are packed with fat. I do not recommend them because of potential chemicals being used on them and the excessive fat. They are greasy, stinky, and not like pork rinds from the days of ole. These are super hard. My dog preferred to bury them instead of eat them. I always default to the wisdom of my dog. He knows what's pure and good.

- Beef neck bones: These are a decent and recommended bone for dogs to enjoy based on their size. For smaller dogs, use chicken or turkey necks, along with bones that are comparable to the meat that was suggested for them to eat in earlier chapters. Common sense is super key here. Matching the natural prey in the wild to the size of your dog is a good way to know the appropriate size of the bone. A bone that is too hard and/or too big could lead to a cracked tooth. Again, we are trying to improve physical and dental health. If we aren't matching natural prey to the size of our dogs, it goes against a species appropriate model.

Never forget the power of being resourceful! Talk to local butchers, or even better, local farmers. Ask them what animal parts they have available. See if you can request or order them. This opens up the option of dehydrating foods to create treats. You can dehydrate tracheas and other strips of meat. Puppies love those! These make great chews! As you read earlier, always watch your dog when he is enjoying a chew treat. If they get too tiny and especially if you have a gulper that tends to just swallow, toss them in the garbage before they get too tiny. You do not want your dog to experience an obstruction in his throat or accidentally choke on the treat.

Over the years, you've probably noticed how training treats have changed. Today, it's fairly easy to find high-end expensive treats. You can easily buy freeze-dried meat or dehydrated treats, though you do want to consider the costs. If you use them, use them few and far between. Read all labels. Look for the minimal fat percentage. It's better to give your dog something with 5% minimal fat than something with 20%. Again, the wild prey an animal would be eating is no more than 3-5% fat content for the whole rabbit, for example. Companies that make treats love to slip in lots of fat for taste and cost efficiency. Also, read the ingredients. It should only be meat. If it has words you can't pronounce or anything other than meat, like preservatives, it is not acceptable for a species appropriate diet.

I highly recommend homemade dehydrated treats, especially chicken liver/heart or beef. I personally don't give them to my dog because I put a lot of time and effort into my dog's food. Since he is an older trained dog, we do a small snack here and there. This is based on whatever he is having that day. He is more than happy with that! I didn't set him up to be majorly driven by treats, but he is my snack boy.

When it comes to training treats, the key word is training. These are to be used to help with behavior modification. Its implementation should be part of a strategic reward system.

Can you use meat treats on plant days? Not if you want to have a species appropriate diet. However, you can use plant treats on plant days. Plant-based training treats are best used for instances when you want to share your approval and happiness because of a specific behavior from your dog. If your dog loves strawberries, that could be a treat reserved for unique occasions on fruit days. Plant foods can be used to reinforce behaviors, depending on your dog's preferences. What about meat? If your dog deals with severe issues concerning his behavior, then you can give a treat that matches the category for that day. So for meat day, give dehydrated meat treats. It's best and easier to train them on meat days. This is a bit of a juggling act because it's not ideal. Still, if you need to round a corner with his behavior, it can be worth it in the short term. Remember, the goal is to not have any meat touch plants in his or her stomach. This means that treats should match the particular food category day.

When my boy was first starting out with this way of feeding, he was traumatically scared of storms and Fourth of July fireworks. I would watch to see when it was going to thunder and move his feeding around that time. I fed him at the start of the storms, using his favorite items in that day's category. Sure enough, within a month, he was starting to train out of it entirely. After eleven years of fear, panting, shaking, and sometimes biting me because he was so scared of the strong noises, it's a different story now. From that transition on, he sleeps upside down next to me through both storms and fireworks. It has been such a huge relief for us both. Sometimes, he even flops on me to get his snuggles. I would have never believed that this was possible for him if I didn't experience it myself. He also sleeps in a much more relaxed and content way. His tummy is happy and full. He is very doggy-zen on meat days and super chill. It's the best!

Why Is My Dog Trying to Eat Non-Foods?

"What on earth are you trying to eat?" Have you ever blurted that out loud when you discovered your dog chowing down on something that is not food? If so, this section is for you.

Pet owners who notice that their pets have an unusual eating habit such as eating socks, rocks, or feces may worry about their pet's health. The concern is not unfounded as these objects can cause damage or even life-threatening blockages in the pet's intestines. This eating behavior is called pica (The Humane Society of the United States, 2010). In humans, pica is a psychological disorder.

Pica is the consumption of non-food items with no significant nutritional value. It occurs mostly in dogs. It's less common in cats. For instance, when a dog eats dirt, it is considered to be a manifestation of pica disorder (Peralta, 2020).

A variety of theories have been floated by experts as to why pica occurs in dogs. However, there is currently insufficient evidence to prove or disprove these theories (The Humane Society of the United States, 2010).

Here is some context. A variety of waste is produced by the animal agriculture industry. What do they do with that waste? If at all possible, they sell it to get rid of it and produce revenue. It's a win/win for them, and the purchaser gets a cheap deal on a raw material. Animal products can be present in a variety of goods. These include, but are not limited to, plastic bags, car and bike tires, fabric softener, fireworks, crayons, cigarettes, paper products, and even toothpaste (Alvarado, 2020) (Sterbenz, 2014).

It's not surprising that dogs can be attracted to such a wide variety of items. They can smell the animal products. The smell of these products confuses your dog. They're not sure what's really food and what isn't because of the smell. Paper products remind dogs of tree bark, so it makes sense that some dogs will be attracted to paper. Refuse to guilt-trip your dog. If your dog eats non-food items, the first step is to put any potentially tempting items out of reach. Additionally, you can either choose to feed them a bit more or redirect them to something that is chewable and safe.

During the transition from your dog's old diet to the species appropriate diet, your dog may have withdrawal symptoms. If you've ever switched to a strict food plan, you can probably relate. For example, if you've ever tried the popular keto diet, then you know that sugar withdrawal is not easy. Some dogs may experience a bit of restlessness during the transition, as it's new territory and their bodies may feel somewhat disoriented at first. This discomfort may create motivation for them to eat non-food items. During this phase, my dog got bouts of crazed super-energy. Regardless of your dog's response, the transitional phase is temporary, so don't worry. For some dogs, the transition is seamless. Others may struggle. It's possible your dog may be eating or attempting to eat non-food items because he is genuinely hungry. If you think that is what's going on, increase the portion sizes by an ounce with meat. Going too fast can create burping, gas, and reflux issues in certain dogs. With plants, add an ounce or two until you find the right amount. Items like dates, bananas, and mangoes tend to put on or level out weight in the same way as adding an extra ounce or two of food. Quinoa gives your dog all the essential amino acids and creates fullness for a long period of time.

Why Does My Dog Eat Grass?

If you've ever taken your dog for a walk or a potty break, only to discover she was chowing down on grass when you weren't looking, here's what you need to know.

Dogs eat grass. So do wolves and coyotes. It's a common, normal behavior. My dog loves to bite and eat grass. He also likes to throw grass around when we play catch. There are varying theories as to why dogs eat grass, that aren't related to my boy being silly. These include:

1. The most common theory is that your dog is having digestive issues (aka upset stomach). Dogs are unable to digest grass. Often, they vomit the grass back up. Eating grass is a method of ridding toxins from their bodies. Essentially, some dogs eat grass so they can throw up and get what's inside their stomach out. Not all dogs vomit after eating grass.
2. Your dog needs more chlorophyll is another theory, although there is little to no documented scientific evidence. We do know that grass contains chlorophyll and that chlorophyll replenishes red blood cells. There are also other health benefits from chlorophyll, such as protecting cells from damage and fighting infections (Gagne, 2020). On the species appropriate plan, the good news is that your dog's body will get sufficient chlorophyll because of the veggies that he will be eating. Grasses are also filled with other nutrients like minerals.
3. If a dog is consuming grass, it doesn't necessarily mean that their diet lacks essential nutrients. It's possible that the behavior is simply instinctual. This action reflects the dog's genetic heritage as omnivores and is an inherent trait passed down through generations of dogs, going back to wolves. (Meyers, 2022). Based on my research, it's my belief that the main motivation for eating grass is instinct.
4. There are smaller theories floating around. These include everything from your dog feeling bored to the idea that perhaps your dog wants or needs more fiber. The good news is that on the species appropriate diet, your dog will receive sufficient fiber. The boredom? Well, get out and play with her! It's good for both of you. I would argue from pure common sense that dogs also get soil and soil-based probiotics, which help their digestive tract.

I know my dog eats grass out of habit and hunger sometimes too, because he tends to do it on fast days. He is used to eating three to four times a day on plant days and three to four times on meat days. He doesn't eat grass every week. It's only occasional. When I tell him he doesn't need to eat grass, he usually looks at me with an "Okay mom" and stops.

Eating grass is typical canine behavior. There is generally no cause for alarm or concern. However, when your dog eats grass, you still must be vigilant and careful. You want to ensure the grass does not contain chemicals or toxins. These will most likely be present if pesticides, herbicides, or fertilizers have been used. In subdivisions, there may be runoff from local fields. You might have to do a little investigative work because some of those items may need to be worked through to ensure safety.

CHAPTER 10

How Do I Determine the Proper Weight for My Dog?

IT'S POSSIBLE THAT YOUR DOG will slim down looking less inflamed and less puffy as lymph starts moving, but they should not be skinny or too skinny. With less fat, grain, fillers, and chemicals in the diet, it only stands to reason that your dog will lose some weight, not in a weight loss way, but in a trimming, firming, muscling way.

Most dogs are overweight just like their owners are. This happens more in the U.S. than in other countries. This is because we feed our pets as we feed ourselves, but it's also from feeding incorrect diets to them and ourselves, which breeds inflammation and stagnant lymph, and eventually dogs and people are tagged with disease titles like autoimmune diseases, which are driven by inflammation. Now, we enjoy our dogs, happiness, excitement and enthusiasm, so we give them another treat. Those add up. If we cannot control or choose not to control our eating, then we don't think there are any issues with our dogs' weight.

Here are a couple of statistics and quotes that may be surprising to learn. Over one-third of adults in the U.S. are classified as obese, with a total of 36.5% of the adult population meeting this criteria. Additionally, 32.5% of American adults are considered overweight. This means that collectively, more than two-thirds of U.S. adults are overweight or obese (O'Rourke, 2020). In fact, having excess body weight, or obesity, has been shown to be associated with over 60 chronic medical conditions. If you are overweight or obese, your likelihood of developing a wide range of medical afflictions and disorders, including cardiovascular disease, cancer, Type 2 diabetes, cerebrovascular accidents, and numerous other illnesses, is markedly elevated (Holland, 2020). The majority of the countries in the rest of the world are less obese than people in the U.S. (World Population Review, 2020).

Back to dogs, people have grown conditioned by constantly seeing overweight domesticated dogs. They think it's just normal, not realizing that the extra weight (and toxicity) is creating disease. As such, that makes a slender dog stand out. Think about wolves and wild dogs. They did not have the luxury or option of being overweight. To survive, which is their primary objective, they had to be lean and in shape. Domesticated dogs that are fed commercialized dog feed daily live a life of ease and convenience. A domesticated dog's lifestyle is not a luxury, though. Honestly, it's a health liability.

Have you heard of agility trainers? Agility is a sport for dogs. During the sport, the dog runs through an obstacle course. It's a competitive race focusing on accuracy and timing. Trainers in this niche usually advocate for the last two ribs on your dog to be easy to see. The belief is that it prevents injury during training and the race. Some dog breeds do not have the last two ribs visible, even though they are healthy and not overweight. As you can imagine, dogs who undergo training for this sport achieve very lean and strong bodies. This is due, in part, because they have a strategic training schedule and because they're not being overfed or fed low-quality meals.

On the suggested species appropriate meal, most dogs will lose weight and get to a lean, healthy state when moderate exercise is also present. For some dogs, their last two ribs will be visible. For others, they will not. For this topic, there's not a one-size-fits-all answer. Dog bodies come in a variety of natural shapes and sizes, just like people do. It's not a sign of health to hold weight, so as their bodies heal, the weight will melt down.

One visible sign that most humans are in shape is that they do not have any areas of skin that extend outward from the hips and hang over, commonly known as "love handles." These are visible signs of excess fat accumulation. However, using this general rule of thumb to your dog is not apples to apples. While people do get pudgy around the middle very easily, dogs do not. If your dog does not have an hourglass shape, generally that is a sign that your dog is overweight. Once again, this can depend on the breed of dog.

Determining the ideal weight of your dog can be a bit tricky. There are a lot of conflicting opinions and information. Know this: your dog's waist should be concave. His waist should also be visible when you're looking down at him. A dog that has her ideal weight will have an abdomen tucked up when you look at it from a side angle. The abdomen should be much higher than the height of the ribcage.

"My dog's weight checks out and looks good, but something is still off." I hear this from time to time. This means that, despite how your dog looks, there are still symptoms of some sort present. Generally, this means your dog is overweight. These health symptoms could be signs that she is consuming too much food. If your dog has zero symptoms and her body and personality all check out and look good, that is evidence that her weight is fine.

On the species appropriate plan, dogs usually lose weight. The proper feeding makes this happen naturally. And of course, if you're implementing a fasting day, that decreases food and fat intake. If you are ever concerned that your dog is too skinny, you can increase the amount of food. The types and categories of food must be in line with this specific plan, of course. If a dog has problematic or impaired digestion, it could be that its body cannot support proper reserves. When this happens, fasting and less food will help. This truly gives the dog's digestive tract the priceless opportunity to heal and recover.

What Can You See While Your Dog Is Detoxing?

Detoxification is the process of removing toxic substances or qualities from a body. Whether it's a human or a dog, there can be symptoms. This is normal. The body is restoring and repairing itself. It's a beautiful thing, despite being possibly somewhat uncomfortable. The transition to this plan will prompt a detox. It's possible that the detox will produce symptoms, although they're most likely going to be minimal or mild. Generally, the younger the dog, the easier the transition. The less drugs, vaccinations, and preventatives that were taken translates into less detox symptoms.

The body is working toward arriving at a new normal. When you go from a toxic diet plan to a healthy one, the wastes that have been stored are released into the bloodstream. Then, the body, in its inherent wisdom, seeks to eliminate the wastes and toxins via eliminative organs. These are the liver, kidneys, lungs, intestines, and skin. The largest is the skin. While exiting the body, the body may experience one or more of the following (or possibly other symptoms): ear issues or infection, inflamed skin, discharge from the eyes (such as mucus, yellow-green pus, or a watery discharge), or general tiredness.

Additionally, you may notice that your dog coughs or hacks. Its urine may smell stronger than usual, which is proof that toxins are exiting. It's possible he may smell bad or have other skin irritations. It is all part of the process. The detox is necessary for health and wellness to be restored. Give your dog extra love, attention, and patience during this transitional time. If you stick with this diet, it's likely he will never deal with those symptoms again. For a few dog owners, it is possible your dog will exhibit zero symptoms, especially if they are younger or less toxic. On these tough days, let them rest and love them extra. By the next day they should be running stronger than ever. If my boy and I ever had a day like this, or if we run too much, we read and snuggle as much as possible. He is stronger for it all around.

If you find that symptoms are still occurring a few months into the new diet plan, then revisit the plan in detail. Symptoms will become less and less as they heal and you can visually see them heal. Make sure that you are following the plan to the letter. Confirm that you are being consistent and not adding anything with toxins or chemicals by accident. Also, confirm that your dog is not eating or gnawing on anything toxic. Finally, if all of that checks out, the symptoms possibly mean that you are feeding your dog too much fat or too large of portions. In that case, you need to reduce the amount of fat consumption or portions on the menu.

During the transition, your dog will be eating more plants than usual or perhaps more than ever. This means she is getting water through the plants. If you notice that she is drinking less water, simply know that it is because of the plant intake. This may mean that your dog urinates more than usual. Sometimes she may urinate a lot more during detox times. In those cases, doggie doors are great, or take extra walks during the week.

If you ever notice a little blood in the urine, do not immediately panic. I believe that can be the body working things out. The body is working to get to a new normal—a healthier new normal! During this time, the body may be dealing with multiple toxins and issues. Therefore, it stands to reason that there may be some irritation or even inflammation in the urinary tract. Most likely that is the source of the small bits of blood in the urine. Most likely, this issue will resolve itself naturally in a few days. If not, then by all means, look into it.

My little guy had bladder leaks six or seven times in the first year. If he hung out the window barking or scuffed blankets, his bladder would fail and leak a little. I knew his bladder was irritated due to toxins leaving his body. During those instances, with just a couple days on this diet, he was restored and back to normal. Each time, he came back stronger than ever. This has been the case with all of his detoxes. Each detox caused him to be extremely tired for a few days in a row. There were also some mood changes and skin issues too. Those have always healed and been resolved.

Is vomiting or diarrhea part of detox? The answer is no. This means your dog is experiencing digestive problems with something on the menu. Dogs vomit because they eat something they cannot digest. The body wants to protect itself, and vomiting is the fastest way to eliminate the problem. Keep note of the foods you're feeding and when vomiting or diarrhea occurs. Try to get to the root cause and put your detective hat on. If your dog's stools aren't normal or they do not seem to be able to effectively digest meat following a meat day, one solution is to feed more bone. Dogs can also vomit for overfeeding, especially the smaller they are. Their tums can only hold so much so if I ever overfed him, he would throw up the precise amount of overage. Luckily, I noticed what I was doing. He is a very sensitive dog, so he needs his food weighed. Even one ounce over can cause issues like gas, bloating, or even vomiting for some dogs. It depends how compromised their digestion may or may not be. Also, the more he does light to moderate exercise, the better his digestion. Adding more bone to the nutritious plan will enlarge and solidify the stools for most dogs. Double-check to see if you have added too much liver to his menu. Too much liver can cause loose stools. The other option would be to add a straight digestive enzyme supplement to assist in breaking down the foods. This is only a temporary measure.

It's not for the rest of his life. The supplements are generally inexpensive, and you can easily find them in pet stores or online. If you try that and your dog is still experiencing symptoms, the next step would be to do an all-plant diet for four to six weeks or as long as required. This can help your dog's digestive tract heal. It should also set the stage for him to produce enough acid to be able to digest meat.

A final caution is to not serve cooked plant foods that are hot or too warm if you must cook, although, recall, to be truly species appropriate you would not cook plant items either. The heat from the cooked item can potentially cause your dog to vomit, and sometimes the entire meal. Some dogs are even slightly heat sensitive food wise. Ideally, serve them at room temperature or cooler.

Can Remedies Be Used to Ease Any Discomfort While Your Dog Heals and Should They Be Used?

This is a valid question. You love your dog. That last thing you want is for her to experience any pain or discomfort. It is possible that your dog may need several weeks up to a few months to heal once you start this diet plan. I have not seen that there is an average to tell you. In light of that, it's natural to ask if there are remedies that can alleviate any symptoms or discomfort during the transition. Overall, dogs itching their skin seems to be the number-one discomfort and annoyance.

I rarely recommend any remedies, not even so-called natural ones. Anything your dog ingests is going to come out of his body in some way, whether it is out the rear end or through the skin. Wastes are visitors, not permanent residents in your dog's body. The longer wastes and toxins stay, the longer they diminish or hurt your dog's overall health. The only one that comes to mind that should be safe is coconut oil. You can directly put it on your dog's skin, and it will cause no harm. Granted, if your dog jumps on your furniture or rubs against your clothes, it's possible the coconut oil may cause a stain. If you choose to administer a natural remedy, proceed with extreme caution.

Will My Dog's Poop or Pooping Habits Change While on This Diet?

Yes. The first change is that if you're switching from commercialized pet feed to a species appropriate diet, the first and most obvious difference is that the poop will have a different look. On plant day, it's usually a lot more than you normally see. This is because your dog's digestive tract is healing.

If the poop turns gray or whitish after a day or so, there's no cause for alarm. This color is related to bone material's calcified remnants. These were not able to be digested, which is normal. In fact, you should want to see poop in this color, especially following meat days, then you will know you're giving enough bone. The other difference is that on meat days, the poop itself will most likely be solid, compressed, and small.

When it comes to plant poops, these will be different from meat poops. Plants poops will be ample. Usually, they are larger than meat poops. This is because your dog's body does not need all the fiber it has received. On fruit days, I always had the most poops overall initially for the first few months.

If your dog poops slowly, there's no cause to be worried. Slow poops do not mean she is constipated. Sometimes, like your mom probably told you, some things just take more time than others.

CHAPTER 11

Variety and Emotional Feeding

IT MAY SURPRISE YOU TO LEARN that to optimize your dog's health, your feeding times should not follow a regularly set carved-in-stone sequence. For example, some dog owners make brags like, "I feed my dog at 8 a.m. and 6 p.m. every day without fail." Don't be one of them. While you will have set schedules for most of your life and will arrive and leave work usually at the same time every day, the feeding times for your dog should feature differences and variances. In other words, randomize the feeding times. Why use different feeding times? Simple. It is biologically in line with wolves and wild dogs. Using a variation of feeding times replicates how it was and is for your dog's biological cousins. Doing so mimics the conditions of how they have eaten for centuries.

If you regularly feed your dog at the exact same hours, then you already know that you've conditioned your dog. If it's getting close to mealtime, he knows. Some dogs are insistent and whine when it's close to mealtime. Does yours? If so, randomized feeding will reduce or possibly eliminate the typical "I'm so hungry. Please feed me now!" behaviors. I tried this, but my little guy was still able to tell time. However, this will work with most dogs.

Implement variety with:

1. the types of food you feed your dog (food variety)
2. how much food you feed your dog (quantity)
3. the times you feed your dog (schedule)

As you read earlier, wild dogs and wolves endured lives of feast or famine. When there was food, they gorged. When there was no prey, they either didn't eat or searched for plants they could eat. Their eating schedule was mixed up and all over the place. This nutrition plan mimics the circumstances in which wolves and wild dogs have eaten plants in the past.

What's interesting and helpful is that these randomly given feedings make it easier for your dog to fast. The randomization means your dog does not know when he will be fed next. This gives her an incentive to eat what is placed in the food bowl, even if it's plants, fruits, or a mixture of both. When my dog is coming off his fast days, he eats what he needs, even if I test him with a big bowl of food, which he will finish later as needed. It's nice to see him taking what he needs.

Beware of Emotional Feeding and Its Impact on Your Dog's Health

Whether we like it or not, our emotions and the emotions of others can influence how we act, think, and live. This is why there are so many books about keeping our emotions in check and building our emotional intelligence. What's wild is that your dog can potentially use your emotions against you. You already know how this works too.

- You're eating a large meat pizza late at night, watching a movie with your family. Your dog has already eaten. The enticing smell is driving your dog crazy. He is whining horribly. You feel bad because you're enjoying a wonderful food and your dog isn't, so you cave in and give your dog extra food. It is true: this is not a good idea overall, but in the first few months when you transition your dog, do note that this whining may be hunger. Broken gastrointestinal tracts, as they heal, sometimes need more food, especially on plant days, as dogs learn how to fast and plant foods digest more quickly. You will have to observe because your dog could really be hungry, and you should feed him in that case. But not pizza, of course.

- There's a horrible thunderstorm, and your dog is scared. Nothing you do seems to calm her down. You decide to try and distract her with a meat treat.

There are countless unending scenarios like those playing out in houses all day, every day.

Keep in mind that dogs are opportunistic feeders. This means their instinct is to take advantage of any and all feeding opportunities as they arise. Whining, putting on a show, or acting out does not mean your dog is genuinely hungry. It simply means he knows food is present, and he wants to eat it.

Breaking off the plan by adding extra treats or any food that is not on the plan hurts your dog's health. It can stop or hinder the progress your dog's body is making toward optimized health.

Your dog mostly lives in a world of conditioned behaviors and routine. Wild dogs and wolves lived in environments with countless variables, struggles, and surprises. If a wolf was hungry, it had to leave the rustic comfort of its den and go hunt. Effort was required. It took a lot of energy, and there were no guarantees that any prey would be found. A wolf never knew if its next feeding was going to be in the next 10 minutes or 10 days. By reading this, it's clear that your dog is not worried or stressed out about going days without food.

Compared to wild dogs and wolves, our dogs are living lives of luxury! Your dog's conditioned behaviors come into play when you're in the kitchen or when you open a pantry door. It could be any trigger. That's possibly when the whining starts. Remember, whining does not mean he is truly hungry. It's just those opportunistic feeder tendencies coming out. Sometimes, if you don't have the correct meat and percentages, they can be hungry when adjusting to the new diet.

After six months, most are adjusted. It can be somewhat easy for dog owners' emotions to influence how they feed their pooch, so it's worth mentioning because it can be positive and negative.

Healthy people eat clean diets. They eat in response to hunger. They know that being hungry is normal. It's not horrible or unpleasant. It's simply a biological reminder that it's time to eat. This is most likely exactly what it's like for dogs as well. You literally know they cannot be hungry and yet they're whining or begging. That's just the opportunistic feeder instinct kicking in. Do not fall for it. However, always observe your dog to make sure that's it. It could be that they need their water refilled or they need to go outside. Observation and really knowing your dog's needs are key.

Many people grew up as emotional eaters. "I'm sad. Let's eat!" "I'm happy. Let's eat!" "I've had a bad/great day. Let's eat!" Maybe you can relate? Emotional eating can rule our lives if we allow it too. As such, an emotional eater who owns a dog will be very tempted to feed his dog in alignment with his emotions (which can be all over the place). Allowing your emotional eating to impact your dog's health negatively is something we all must avoid.

Do not let your emotions hurt your dog's health. Likewise, if you sense you need professional help, there is no shame in looking for assistance. Every human being deals with a variety of inner and outer obstacles throughout life. The assistance can be positive for you both. After all, you're your dog's whole life. They depend on you for their daily health and happiness.

For humans and canines alike, for the majority, it's not agonizing, stressful, or dire to have an empty stomach. Some people and dogs are more sensitive though, so if you have a dog like that you will need to adjust not to cause undue stress, or even undue potential weight loss. For wild dogs and wolves, an empty stomach does not always compel them to go hunting in an instant, either. They're used to empty stomachs. They're conditioned to go days without eating. It's perfectly fine for your dog to have an empty stomach. Now, we're talking about dogs in the wild here and theoretically, if you want to maintain a species appropriate diet, following the wisdom of their ancestors, you should do what it says above. However, when transitioning from commercialized pet feeds and potentially changing a dog's feeding schedule, it can definitely stress out certain dogs as mentioned above. Note: if you have a dog that is sensitive, prone to stress, older and/or inflexible, give your dog grace during the transition. If they don't adjust fairly quickly, stressing your dog out for the sake of maintaining a rigid feeding schedule is not in your dog's best interest. For health reasons, as we've stated, it is best to follow a species appropriate feeding schedule, but not if it dramatically stresses out your dog. Again, stress can certainly damage your dog's health. Being flexible and using common sense is the best overall choice here. In that instance, you do what you can and meet your dog some place in the middle or make the transition double the time. I have seen folks stick to rigid schedules or plans just to stick to them at the peril of the dog, and we are trying to optimize health, nutrition and keep them around as long as possible, but they should be happy, non-stressed and pain free, and there is never a situation, even when detoxing, that your dog should be underweight.

Here are some good tips.

First, remember that the goal is to optimize your dog's health. One, getting as close to a species appropriate diet is good for that. Two, stressing out your dog isn't. Breaking off from the plan can slow the healing process, but it's best to transition on your dog's timeline with reasonable accommodation. Put yourself in your dog's shoes or maybe in this case paws, well that doesn't necessarily translate, but you get the idea.

Second, you might find an accountability partner or friend who deals with emotional eating so you can work together to overcome that obstacle if you feel it can impact your dog's wellbeing.

Third, do not be the dog owner who loves her dog to death. Overfeeding your dog is not love. Feeding anything toxic will impact your dog's vitality and health and set the stage for disease. You can also underexercise your dog as well. When my dog was healing, I thought it was better to carry him up and down the stairs. We got to a point where I'd sit him down and he would not want to walk in the yard. We started running sessions together and he was fine again and his muscles were functioning well. This is something to watch out for in older and/or small dogs as muscle structure can be lost quicker. Having them exercise is a good thing, and it certainly does not have to be high intensity. It's very good for their lymph system.

Fourth, it's always best to choose to love yourself, and that will transition to loving your dog. Love is strong. It sets and maintains reasonable boundaries. It's always looking out for the best interest. Put your focus there, and great things will come about for you and your pets.

To summarize, you're the informed owner now. Choose to stay on-plan with reasonable considerations as needed. Baby steps are still steps to reach an end goal. You're still getting there, even if you have to take a step back to move forward. Stay flexible. Only deviate with more foods if needed or seasonal (my boy likes certain foods at certain times of year, but also enjoys the predictability of meals on certain days as he memorizes them), as you observe your dog or as they get tired of a certain food. If they are running around starving and thin, don't stick to the metric just to stay on a plan; please let common sense prevail and feed them. So don't ignore whining and hunger, validate it with what you observe. You will create such an amazing relationship with your dog that you will know when they voice their opinions and what they are saying. Dogs that exercise more definitely need more food for weight maintenance and for more energy. You do have to feed them more. Any metrics or numbers given are just starting points.

You cannot find your true percentage for your dog without carefully observing their body, weight, and overall health (i.e., shiny moisturized coat, shiny moist nose, sparkling eyes, bright white teeth, to name a few). Determine which feeding example works for you and your dog. Then, feed according to the plan that's best for your dog. Follow a schedule consistently that's best for both of your interests. You can also choose to use it as a basis and adapt it to your pet's best feeding schedule or plan, which I highly encourage you to do. Everything I give you is a starting point. You can customize it to your dog's unique needs, age, physical level, and exercise levels. All these things make a difference, which is why nobody can tell you how much to truly feed your dog or how you should feed your unique dog. My dog loves consistency. No matter how many times I tried in the past to stick to a plan, it was best to stick to his plan for both of us. It did not detract from his healing or health whatsoever. Do not be guilt-tripped or shamed by others into feeding your dog a certain way. Work hand in hand with your dog. Get to know him in a more communicative way, and I assure you that if you're observing properly, you will be able to find and solve any problems to your dog's benefit and yours. If you're noticing your dog exhibiting certain undesirable behaviors, see if a little increase or decrease in food solves the issue. The answer could also lie in more exercise or more rest. Again, observation, observation, observation. You have been given scenarios so you can know when to fast. During these times, your dog's body can devote all its energies to healing. You're now ready to remove the burden off your dog's body so your best friend can start to heal. Remember, there are no one-size-fits-all nutrition plans for dogs … no absolute feed schedules, no absolute exercise schedules, no absolute potty break schedules, no absolute sleep schedules, no absolute rest schedules, and so on. Every dog is its own unique individual with its own personality and emotions, just like us. There are calm dogs, energetic dogs, and more easy-going dogs. Each will adjust differently on its own schedule. If you truly love your dog, you'll respect their own individuality and work with them to achieve any goal, never against them. You can only learn what type of dog you have by proper communication and observation.

CHAPTER 12

Puppies and a Species Appropriate Diet

PUPPIES ARE THE BEST, AREN'T THEY? We want to give our absolute best to our pups. We can set the stage for health and wellness for the rest of their lives.

As you can imagine, dog pups and wolf pups share many similarities. From their feeding habits to their crazy playfulness, it's easy to see how they're related (Gander, 2020) (International Wolf Center, n.d.). This connection further demonstrates how much our puppies can benefit from having a diet that's more in line with what wolves consume in nature. This chapter will mostly present new information for puppy diets.

Additionally, it will end with information and insights about puppies from earlier parts of the book. This way, you have everything about puppies in one chapter.

How Fast Will My Puppy Grow?

Puppies grow at different rates depending on the breed. While puppies are considered adult dogs at one year old, their bones are still developing and they continue to grow in height and size for anywhere between 6 to 24 months (Paretts, 2019). Bigger breeds spend more time in the puppy stage. Smaller breeds require less time in the puppy stage. For example, a German shepherd requires around 3 full years before being out of the puppy and juvenile stages (Reardon, n.d.). In contrast, chihuahuas only take about 10 to 12 months to reach adulthood (Dog Food Smart, 2020).

To learn about your specific breed's growth, I advise doing an online search for "puppy growth chart," "puppy chart," and "puppy's adult weight." Add the name of your breed in the search bar to narrow your results. Know that the research on this topic is varied.

What About Vaccinations and Titers?

If you're properly raw feeding your puppy, you don't need vaccinations.

Concerning titers, after your puppy has received its first round of vaccinations, it's best to perform a titer test. This is especially true if you've only given one or two vaccinations, with the last one given after 16 weeks of age. If a titer test is conducted a few weeks later, it can determine how effective the vaccinations were in conferring immunity. The test results are useful because if there's any measurable titer to the disease, then the goal of conferring immunity has been achieved. A positive result is all that's needed to show that the puppy has developed immunity to the viruses that were introduced via vaccination. As a result, you can confidently avoid further vaccinations for your pet, which has now become immune for life (Falconer, 2020).

If you're pro vaccinations, here is one of the latest protocols with less toxic outcomes and reactions due to the vaccination schedule, by Dr. Jean Dodds. She is a top holistic veterinarian who is well-known both nationally and internationally.

"The following vaccine protocol is offered for those dogs where minimal vaccinations are advisable or desirable. The schedule is one I recommend and should not be interpreted to mean that other protocols recommended by a veterinarian would be less satisfactory. It's a matter of professional judgment and choice."

From her research and experience as a well-known, top holistic veterinarian nationally and internationally, Dr. Dodds suggests this schedule:

9–10 weeks of age
Distemper + Parvovirus, MLV
e.g., Merck Nobivac (Intervet Progard) Puppy DPV

14–15 weeks of age
Distemper + Parvovirus, MLV

18 weeks of age
Parvovirus only, MLV

Note: New research states that the last puppy parvovirus vaccine should be at 18 weeks old.

20 weeks or older, if allowable by law
Rabies—give 3–4 weeks apart from other vaccines, mercury-free (thimerosal-free, TF)

1 year old
Distemper + Parvovirus, MLV
This is an optional booster or titer. If the client intends not to booster after this optional booster or intends to retest titers in another three years, this optional booster at puberty is wise.

1 year old
Rabies—give 3–4 weeks apart from other vaccines
3-year product if allowable by law; mercury-free (TF)

"Perform vaccine antibody titers for distemper and parvovirus every three years thereafter, or more often, if desired. Vaccinate for rabies virus according to the law, except where circumstances indicate that a written waiver needs to be obtained from the primary care veterinarian. In that case, a rabies antibody titer can also be performed to accompany the waiver request." (Dodds, 2017).

If you have concerns about vaccine toxicity and prefer natural immunity, you might be wondering if you can vaccinate your dog once and be done with it. Schultz conducted a study on this topic. His research, including studies on his own dogs and controlled studies, suggests that core vaccines that protect against life-threatening diseases provide immunological memory for at least seven years, except for rabies, which is typically effective for three years. While he recommends vaccinating against rabies every three years, as mandated by most states, he advises a more conservative approach for the other essential vaccines, with no more frequent than once every three years (Schultz, 2003).

The 2017 Canine Vaccine Guideline by AAHA still recommends a series of Canine Distemper Vaccines (CDV), but in small print, they state that a single dose of a combination vaccine given to dogs over 20 weeks old when presented for initial vaccination in high-risk settings is expected to provide protective immunity, according to the AAHA 2017 Canine Vaccine Guideline (Ford et al., 2017). It is noteworthy that the AAHA highlights the final statement in bold. This may feel like a red flag to most people, leading them to wonder why certain traditional veterinarians are not adhering to these guidelines, and it should.

The AAHA guidelines provide valuable information for veterinary staff to improve the health of pets by addressing essential issues and performing necessary tasks. However, it is unclear why vaccination protocols are not being utilized relative to the items that influence the patient's susceptibility to health problems, stage of life, and way of living in their environment. In my personal experience, I have not seen any veterinarian utilize the Lifestyle-Based Vaccine Calculator. Its purpose is to help veterinary teams recommend vaccinations based on the patient's unique circumstances and lifestyle considerations. It incorporates reference tables that are quick and straightforward to use for dogs in private ownership and those residing in public animal shelters. It utilizes algorithms for testing antibodies and tips for patients who are late for their vaccination schedule. It also includes information on compliance and exemptions regarding rabies, overviews of immunotherapeutic treatments, instructions for proper vaccine storage and handling, and additional capabilities (Ford, et al., 2017). Despite being included in the AAHA guidelines, my veterinarian has never discussed titers or based my dog's vaccine schedule on all the aforementioned factors, nor are shelters titering before vaccinating. As a concerned pet parent, I hope to raise awareness so that others can make informed decisions for their pets.

If your dog's titer shows immunity, you can use it as proof when requested or to avoid unnecessary vaccinations. There are other alternatives to vaccination such as pet-sitting, hiring a dog walker, or having a family member care for your pet while you are away. Some clinics take pets out to the woods for natural immunity and never vaccinate. There are various ways to prioritize your dog's health and wellness.

Feeding Puppies a Species Appropriate Diet

To ensure optimal growth, it is recommended that puppies be fed 2-3% of their expected adult weight, or 0.02 to 0.03 as a decimal, which would be 2 to 3 units of that portion out of 100%. This is divided into multiple meals throughout the day, based on their age, or 4% to 6% of their current weight (Raw Fed Dogs, n.d.). As puppies reach 4-6 months of age, they require more food and additional edible bone to support the development of their adult teeth. During this period, it's crucial to monitor the puppy's weight and ensure that they are not becoming underweight, as their energy needs are high due to their growing teeth.

Puppies require more than twice the amount of calcium compared to adult dogs at a maintenance level. Large-breed puppies, in particular, require close monitoring of the levels and ratios of calcium and phosphorus in their diets to prevent the risk of developmental orthopedic disease (Savory Prime Pet, n.d.). It is essential to provide a balanced diet that includes appropriate plant-based foods to ensure that puppies receive these important minerals.

Summary of Salient Points Relative to Puppies

Below, I will recap what you have read about puppies in all the previous chapters.

- In a healthy pup, bacteria and germs are irrelevant. So is genetics. Even if your pet has certain negative genes, they can stay turned off by a proper environment and by what you put in and on your pet. The diet is what creates health and healing.
- Puppies need to be weaned on regurgitated food. That's how it's done in the wild. In our everyday environments, it's not possible to replicate and mimic regurgitated foods.
- Lots of research and evidence show that wolves and their pups eat plants.
- If you rotate your puppy's diet, it can help strengthen her digestive tract. This can make it easier for her to digest new proteins, which in turn reduces the likelihood of them experiencing stomach upset (Kim, 2019).
- First-time bone chewers such as puppies should be taught how to eat a bone. Choose a stick-shaped bone such as a turkey neck or beef ribs. Hold one end of the bone and let your dog chew on the other and pull away if it seems like your dog will try to swallow the whole thing! Through this process, much like a mother wolf might, you teach your dog how to patiently enjoy a bone.

- Watch your puppy when she is eating a bone. Too much bone can lead to constipation. The easiest measure is to give the amount of bone that matches the portions from the animal you're feeding. For example, if you want to give your pup a chicken quarter, include that bone from that portion.
- When feeding a puppy, it's usually best to avoid feeding that cute loving ball of energy late at night. Feed him more frequently throughout the day than you would for an adult dog. My little guy actually did require a full tummy to sleep through the night. Again, it's the puppy's choice on this one. Experiment and see what works best!
- Puppies generally love dehydrated tracheas and other strips of dehydrated meat.
- Due to puppies' nutritional needs and growth, it is best not to fast them until after they are at least a year old or well beyond for growth and nutritional purposes.

CHAPTER 13

Cats and a Species Appropriate Diet

DOES THIS DIET WORK FOR CATS? Yes! In general, the content in this book concerning the pet industry and disease relates not only to dogs, but yes, it can also relate to cats. It seemed less thorough not to write about cats, as many dog owners also have cats. Considering that, I chose to share a diet that can keep them healthy and well too. How to feed them is modified, which you'll read more about soon.

The Species Appropriate Diet is simpler for cats because cats are dedicated carnivores. If you remember, dogs are facultative carnivores. This means that, although their preference is meat (prey), dogs can also eat plants. Cats are obligate carnivores. Obligate means "restricted to a particular function or mode of life" (Lexico, n.d.) and "able to exist under only one set of environmental conditions" (Collins Dictionary, n.d.).

For cats, consuming meat is an absolute biological imperative, and there is no alternative to it. It is not possible for a cat to survive on a vegan diet (Gates, 2019). To implement this nutrition plan, remove all plants from the menu. Your cat will exclusively eat meat, organs, and bones.

The preference of cats is food that has been freshly killed. Dogs can easily eat and digest rotting meat. Cats, not so much.

Read this entire chapter before implementing the nutrition plan. There are key details you need to know before making the transition. Older cats are slower to transition. They've lived their lives a certain way for years and so this change will be disorienting. Younger cats and kittens transition more easily.

As with your dog, be patient and willing to adapt as needed. Observe your cat carefully and take mental notes. The benefits will far outweigh any hassles of implementing this nutrition plan.

The action steps below may require days, weeks, or even a few months. There is no set timeframe for cats when transitioning, regardless of their age.

Pre-Transition (Start here if you have been feeding commercialized pet food of any kind.)

The steps to implement the transition are as follows:

1. Before the transition, reduce the quantity of food you're currently feeding your cat.
2. Feed your cat two smaller meals per day. These can be one-half

or one-fourth of what you have currently been feeding him. Do this for three to five days leading up to the transition. Note: If your cat vocalizes due to hunger, it's okay to give a snack, but do not give too much as you're transitioning. If your cat isn't finicky at all or if you have been feeding raw already, you don't have to transition in a more structured way. You want to train your cat not to vocalize, but if it does not bother you, it's fine. The goal is to retrain your cat if you feel it's necessary or your cat prompts it. Feed your cat what she has been recently eating. Since the transition is to raw meat, it's best to add warm water to dry food as a first step. This makes the food moist, which is similar to raw meat. Do not add too much water, or the food will become soggy.

3. Next (before feeding your cat), you want to warm up the food. There are two options. The first and best option is to put the food in a container and let it float. Use hot water. Let it stay there until it gets to body temperature. The second option is to use your microwave to delicately warm up the food (make sure it's in a glass dish, then take it out to feed so the dish does not accidentally burn the cat). Both of these methods help get your cat acclimated to the new normal, which will be meat at body temperature. The typical temperature range for cats falls between 100.4 degrees Fahrenheit and 102.5 degrees Fahrenheit (Pets WebMD, n.d.). Just so you know, body temperature is always higher than room temperature.

4. Have you been feeding your cat high-quality, grain-free kibble? If so, skip this step. If not, moving forward, purchase a better and more nutritious version of kibble. Heat the food as outlined in Step 3 and see if your cat eats it. If she won't eat it, look for a different type of kibble.

Moving to Canned Cat Food (Begin reading here if you have already been feeding canned food)

1. Once your cat has shifted to eating the new kibble, implement canned cat food. If your cat has mostly been eating kibble for its entire life, smash up a few pieces of kibble and put them on top of the canned food. This helps some cats during the transition. If your cat rejects the food, use warm moist kibble and add a little canned food. Increase the amount of the canned food in the kibble over the next few days and weeks. You'll need to work with your cat on this. It may be five days or five weeks, although less finicky cats simply adapt to it. Again, all cats are different just like us. This can go faster or slower depending on the cat. Some cats are just all in! Sometimes the wisdom of the cat just takes over.
2. If your cat eats healthy canned food with no issues, skip to the next step. If your cat rejects canned cat food, here is what to do. Experiment with different brands. This may take some time. You might buy four to eight brands at once (one can of each). Start with the cheaper brands and move up to the more costly ones when attempting to feed him. Take mental notes.
3. Are canned food feedings going well? If so, purchase raw foods that are commercially prepared. In pet food stores, it's usually frozen ground meat. If your cat eats these, you're one step closer to implementing the new nutrition plan. If your cat shuns it, here are options. Add canned food with raw food. Allow the canned food to take precedence in the bowl. Your cat may eat it all, believing it's normal canned food. This may cause some digestive discomfort. At the same time, for some cat owners, it is a necessary step. Over time, start decreasing the canned food amount and increasing the raw food. Take

mental notes and observe your cat's responses. If there are any health issues, move to the next step.
4. To help a finicky feline wean completely off canned food, it can be helpful to try lightly braising the raw meat. You only need to slightly braise the outer part of the food, nothing more. If the cat shuns it, braise it a little more and see if she will accept it. Adding a small amount of warm water can help, too, since most cats like moist food. The goal is raw so only do this during the transition period.

At this point, it's time to move your cat to the new species appropriate raw meat plan! Congratulations!

Species Appropriate Feeding Foods List for Cats

Which raw foods are recommended for your cat? Really, it's any meat your cat enjoys and/or meats that are common where you live. Different locations in the world have access to different regional foods. When you feed bone, keep it species appropriate. This means to use the bone size of the prey that cats would find in the wild. Here are some raw food examples in no particular order:

- buffalo
- chicken (chicken wing bones are consumable, just keep them species appropriate in size relative to what they would eat if they were barn cats, ie. mice, squirrels, chipmunks, etc.)
- fish (including a wide variety; smelt is a great option)
- lean beef
- organ meats (use in moderation)
- quail and game hens (feed a few times a month if you choose, but not daily; these have consumable bones)

- rabbit (use in moderation)
- turkey
- venison

During the final stage of the transition, as mentioned above, it is possible that you may need to lightly cook or braise the raw meat if your cat is not eating. Additionally, you may need to mix the food.

From there, it's simple. Every day is meat day for your cat! I find it best to alternate the meats and do a variety throughout the week (Tollden Farms, n.d.). Rotate the raw diet for your pet, as long as your pet can handle the changes. It's important to offer a variety of protein sources to improve nutrition and well-being, just like with any other type of food. If your pet's raw diet does not include organ meats, it is advisable to add them to the diet a few times per week (Only Natural Pet, 2020). This rotation creates a variety of sources of protein. This allows your cat to consume a wide variety of nutrients. It's all in an effort to optimize his life. As we learned in the wolf chapters, the most nutrient-dense areas of prey are in the internal organs or offal.

Helpful Insights

- Most people follow the PMR model for percentage breakdowns, no matter which model they're using. A nutrient-balanced diet has been most concluded in research to be somewhere near this breakdown: 80% muscle meat (can include hearts), 10% bone, and 10% internal organs (5% is liver). Note that a heart is considered a muscle meat and an internal organ. The majority of animals are around 25% organ meat by weight, so there is justification to move to feeding a variety of internal organs (Scott, 2022). These include eyes, brain, spleen, lung, and so on and can make up 25% of the daily meal, but we also have to consider that just like bobcats in the wild, they are not eating that perfectly balanced meal for every meal. This gives the justification for the 80/10/10 breakdown. If you're looking for perfection, it's probably somewhere in the middle of both. The optimal diet could be 65% to 80% muscle meat, 10% bone, and 10% to 25% internal organs.

- Fasting can be problematic for cats, especially overweight cats. Ongoing fasting in cats, especially ones that are overweight, can cause hepatic lipidosis (Scanlan, 2011). Overall, I do not recommend fasting for cats.
- Body-temperature foods help your cat digest the foods more easily. Once cats' transition, they tend to enjoy foods at body temperature.
- When you're attempting to feed your cat a new food, wipe some of it on his nose or paws. By doing so, your cat must deal with it by licking it off! This helps get them going in the right direction.
- To cut meat or not? If your cat will eat meat that is not cut, let her do so. This is helpful for their dental health. It puts a cat's rear cutting teeth to work. These animals possess eight premolar teeth that are sharp and serrated, allowing them to cut their food into smaller pieces that can be swallowed whole. Additionally, they have four molars that are used for crushing bones (Virbac UK, n.d.). If your cat does not take to whole meat, then it's best (and perfectly healthy) to cut up the meat in bite-size pieces.
- Watch your cat's weight. Unlike dogs, cats regulate their intake and usually do so very well. Observing your cat's weight can help you navigate portion size.

- Do you allow your cat to wander outside? If so, this can be problematic. You do not want your cat getting into another cat's food. Most likely, some cat owners in your neighborhood feed their cats outdoors. If your cat eats another cat's kibble, this hinders optimizing her health. Feed your cat before you allow her to go outside and wander. Another idea is requesting your neighbors feed their cats indoors.
- Raw feeding can cause decreased urination in cats because the meat has moisture. Don't be alarmed if your cat urinates less.

Per day, it is recommended that you feed grown cats 2-3% of their body weight, and kittens 5-7% of their current weight. Keep in mind that these are general guidelines and the amount of food should be adjusted based on exercise levels and age (Tollden Farms, n.d.).

When it comes to feeding kittens, it's important to provide them with enough food to support their growth into adulthood. This will ensure that they have sufficient calcium and other essential nutrients to develop strong bones and maintain good health.

Meats I have fed cats include chicken, quail, beef, venison, pheasant, game hens, turkey, organ meats, and a wide variety of fish.

CHAPTER 14

Resources and More Information

A Few Supplies You Will Need:

1. poultry shears
2. meat cleaver
3. sharp cutting knife
4. optional: Japanese knife

Recommended Products

On the journey to optimizing your dog's health, you will need to purchase certain products from time to time. On my website, I've created a special Recommended Products page. It's a list of products I used while transitioning my dog to the new diet, as well as products I currently use from time to time.

Essentially, it's a tried-and-true list for when you're having a hard time trying to find the best items and solutions. Feel free to bookmark the web page when you land there.

To find the specific brands I use and to see all of the recommended products, go to: wellnessandhealthnow.com/pet-products/

Some helpful items along the journey to dog health and wellness include:

- bone knives
- brushes for dry brushing and lymphatic drainage
- comfortable dog recovery collars to prevent wound-licking from surgery or otherwise
- digestive enzymes
- ear solutions for ear infections
- Epsom salt for soaks
- grinder attachments
- grip wear for dog shoes for hiking and related products
- items for neck wounds, neck bands, T-shirts for UV, pet anxiety, alopecia, onesies, and wound care
- meat and bone grinders
- poultry shears
- topical treatments to calm itchy skin
- troughs for gulpers and fast eaters
- and more

Pet Coaching and Consulting Services

Once you have started the diet and get going, you may find you need more detailed, specific information than what this book offers or need help picking products off the Recommended Products section. You may also decide you can't wait to get started as you have very serious health issues, so I do consultations and pet coaching for those very needs. So, if you find yourself needing detailed coaching and want one-on-one expert guidance, you're welcome to reach out to me. I get great joy from meeting loving pet owners and their babies and even more joy from seeing them go from sick and painful to bouncing and happy!

My website includes a variety of great consultation topics, and we can discuss anything you are struggling with after you have read my book and started the diet with your pet. Items spring to light once you are in the implementation process. Quite frankly, it would be next to impossible for any single book to outline everything concerning your dog and his health.

To inquire about my services, simply send me a message. I'm only an email or social media message away. I would love to serve you as you optimize your dog's health.

You can pay for your 30- or 60-minute service here toward the bottom of this page: wellnessandhealthnow.com/work-with-me/

If you want to learn more, feel free to visit:
wellnessandhealthnow.com/about-the-book
or
wellnessandhealthnow.com/pet-products/
or
facebook.com/dogwellnesscoaching

AFTERWORD

The Rest of the Story...

THEN, HER DOG GOT SICK. It was October 2019. Stephanie went to a specialty clinic for second opinion and a top Veterinary University. She talked with professionals at a top veterinary teaching college, and after much emotional stress, she started to lean toward doing the suggested surgery on her beloved dog. However, she kept coming back to a central problem. She had received contradictory advice and information from the best in the field, plus it was highly lacking in common sense, favoring pain and suffering and surgery rather than love, and enjoyment till the end given both results shared had the same outcome, so she couldn't resolve by way of surgery. It just didn't make sense, and she wanted to do everything possible to protect her boy from more pain and unnecessary suffering.

So given her prior learning in the field and her heavy statistics knowledge, it didn't make sense to her. She was told that, with the many diagnostics and testing, with surgery, she would get three to four months left with her dog. She was also told she would get the same without surgery. She was urged and pressured to move forward with surgery. She was told, "You're going to kill your dog without surgery for sure." Still, the information didn't add up. She didn't know where to turn. What was the best decision? How could she try to heal her dog and keep him healthy and happy? How could she extend his life? How could she stop his pain and suffering and not create more? She needed more information.

Her quest to save her dog's life went into overdrive. She researched for 24 hours straight, rarely sleeping and killing herself for answers that made sense. After all, she was told he needed immediate surgery and she was out of time. It was the first time she had done that in her life. She set up a week's worth of consultations with two of the top holistic veterinarians both nationally and internationally. She booked appointments with the top international homeopathic vet and the top Chinese medicine vet. She shared the diagnostics over and over and got their views. She ended up with five non-surgeries and three surgery suggestions. Still traumatized on making a final decision of whether to do surgery, she sought out one more vet. This vet had been talking about the latest possible holistic and genetic cancer treatments. She felt that he covered all the bases. He suggested non-surgery. So, after talking to endless experts, her tally was that half-recommended surgery and a little over half recommended non-surgery.

Stephanie asked herself, "What's most important to and for my dog? Which decision will make him healthy, happy, pain-free, and non-traumatized?" She found her answer. The discovery was a specific way of feeding called raw feeding. She dove in headfirst into this new world. What was being said, how to feed, how disease was created, and more … it all made logical sense to her. This led her to reading multiple books, researching raw feeding, joining support groups, and more. During this time, she kept rescheduling the surgery. She left it on the books for safekeeping, and then it happened. She started to see her dog heal. It started with him growing a complete full coat of new hair. He also grew hair on his face. That had never been possible due to toxicity. She had never seen what he was supposed to fully look like until he was 11 years old, which saddened her, yet she was thrilled he was healing. Next, her dog became more energetic. He started running and playing again. He was happier too. He went from barely getting upstairs at 11 years old to bouncing up them like when he was young. Other changes happened too. Glowing teeth emerged, gleaming eyes sparkled where he once could barely see, and fatty tumors were nearly gone. Every health issue on the list reversed almost entirely!

It was at that point that she knew that raw feeding had worked for her dog. She saw many other dogs healing in online groups. She felt it was her duty to do what's right and share this information to whomever she could. Her goal is to help dogs and cats bypass suffering, pain, and disease by empowering pet owners with specific raw feeding insights and strategies.

Prior to raw feeding saving her dog's life, Stephanie was a regular responsible dog owner. She followed all the usual rules. She did vaccinations only up to three years old. Then, she moved to titers. Plus, she did the least toxic heartworm pills. (She eventually moved to six months a year only. She didn't like giving her dog drugs. Like most dog owners, she was told that they will get heartworm without them.) On top of that, Stephanie did the annual bloodwork and vet visits to the top clinics. For one clinic, she drove seven hours roundtrip. She fed her dog the most organic pet foods, and he still got sick and was apparently dying, according to the experts. He had both a growth and a tumor. Plus, he was inflamed and allergenic. He licked his paws so badly during certain times of the year and had a pink tummy and little belly hair. She even had him genetically tested, thinking there were some major flaws and bad genes were turned on. There wasn't. He came back literally without any typical breed flaws across the board. There were over 200 genetic abnormalities tested. She then knew it was something she put on or in him, something environmental. Again, it confirmed her suspicions about what created her boy's disease states.

This grueling and gut-wrenching journey led to the creation of this book. This book is written for the love of her dog and for your dogs and cats. It outlines how she saved his life. She and her precious dog ate, slept, biked, walked, and traveled together. Her dog was and is her world.

Stephanie understands what your pets mean to you. She knows you can't bear seeing one sick animal. That's why she wrote her book and continues to share what she learns. She wishes you and your dogs the happiest, healthiest, and most joyful lives possible. As we all know, we get one chance on earth, well in our physical form they say. So, why not live it the absolute best we can and to the fullest? To do that, you must feel your best. So must your dog! He deserves the same. Day in and out, they give us their daily protection, complete trust, love, and adoration. It's a privilege and responsibility to keep them healthy and safe!

REFERENCES

ABC Health & Wellbeing. Staff writers. (2017, May 13). War on waste: *Are fresh veggies always healthier than frozen?* ABC News. abc.net.au/news/health/2017-05-14/ fresh-vs-frozen-vegies/8443310

AKC Staff. (2020, July 16). *Can Dogs Eat Bones?* American Kennel Club. akc.org/expert-advice/nutrition/exercise-caution-when-giving-your-dog-a-bone/

Alvarado, P. (2020, October 8). *9 Everyday Products You Didn't Know Had Animal Ingredients.* Treehugger. treehugger.com/everyday-products-you-didnt-know-had-animal- ingredients-4858750

Ask The Scientists. (n.d.). *Answers to Your Questions About Soy*. https://askthescientists.com/qa/why-does-usana-use-soy

Australian Fitness Academy. (November 15, 2019). *Macronutrients vs. Micronutrients.* https://www.fitnesseducation.edu.au/blog/health/macronutrients-vs-micronutrients

Australian Government Department Of Health. (2013, October 8). *Nutrients*. Australian Government Department Of Health. https://www.health.gov.au/resources/publications/national-healthy-school-canteens-manager-training-parts-1-and-2

B.A.R.F. Basic Ancestral Raw Food. (n.d.). *BARF Vs PMR For Raw-Feeders*. B.A.R.F. Basic Ancestral Raw Food. barfindia.com/blog/barf-vs-pmr-raw-feeders/

Bjarnadottir, A. (2019, June 26). *Is Avocado a Fruit or a Vegetable?* Healthline. healthline.com/nutrition/is-avocado-a-fruit-or-a-vegetable

Bob's Red Mill. (2018, February 1). *Amaranth vs. Quinoa*. Bob's Red Mill. bobsredmill.com/blog/special-diets/amaranth-vs-quinoa/

Bonnaud E., Bourgeois K., Vidal E., Kayser Y., Pascal M., Tranchant Y., Legrand J., Nativel M., Medina F., Bretagnolle V. (August 20, 2007). *Feeding Ecology of a Feral Cat Population on a Small Mediterranean Island*. Journal of Mammalogy. https://academic.oup.com/jmammal/article/88/4/1074/908458

Bosch, G., Hagen-Plantinga, E.A., Hendriks, W.H. (2014, November 21). *Dietary nutrient profiles of wild wolves: insights for optimal dog nutrition?* US National Library of Medicine National Institutes of Health. https://pubmed.ncbi.nlm.nih.gov/25415597/

Bradford, A. (2017, July 10). Wolf Facts: Gray Wolves, *Timber Wolves & Red Wolves*. Live Science. livescience.com/27909-wolves.html

REFERENCES

Bradford, A. (2018, December 04). *Carnivores: Facts About Meat Eaters.* https://www.livescience.com/53466-carnivore.html

Brown, V. C. (2019, March 29). *The Body Was Designed To Heal Itself: A Case Study.* Thrive Global. thriveglobal.com/stories/the-body-was-designed-to-heal-itself-a-case-study/

Buckenmaier III, C. (October 4, 2018). "The doctor of the future will give no medication but will interest his patients in the care of the human frame, diet and in the cause and prevention of disease"—Thomas A. Edison (1847-1931). U.S. Medicine: The Voice of Federal Medicine. https://www.usmedicine.com/editor-in-chief/the-doctor-of-the-future-will-give

Buehler, J. (2020, February 11). Science News. *Wolves regurgitate blueberries for their pups to eat.* sciencenews.org/article/wolves-regurgitate-blueberries-pups-diet

Burrows, W. Professor of Microbiology, University of Chicago. (n.d.). *Disease.* Britannica. britannica.com/science/disease

Cabbagetown Pet Clinic. (2020, March 2). *How Essential Oils Can Affect Your Pet's Health.* Cabbagetown Pet Clinic. cabbagetownpetclinic.com/2020/03/02/how-essential-oils-can-affect-your-pets-health/

CBSH Health. (2020, March 20). *Acute and chronic inflammation.* cbhs.com.au/mind-and-body/blog/acute-and-chronic-inflammation

Cinque, R. C. (n.d.). *Nutrition A Hygienic Perspective - Article #3: Nutrition, A Hygienic Perspective by Ralph C. Cinque, D.C.* Raw Food Explained. rawfoodexplained.com/nutritional-science/ nutrition-a-hygienic-perspective.html

Clark, A. (2017, July 28). *Dog Diseases A-Z: The Pet Symptoms Full List.* Pet Symptoms. petsymptoms.com/dog-diseases-pet-symptoms/

Clark, M. (n.d.). *Is It Okay To Give My Dog A Bone? Which Bones Are Safe For Dogs?* Dogtime. dogtime.com/dog-health/dog-food-dog-nutrition/52539-ok-give-dog-bone-bones-safe-dogs

Cleveland Clinic Website. (n.d.) Autophagy. Cleveland Clinic. https://my.clevelandclinic.org/health/articles/24058-autophagy

Collins Dictionary. (n.d.). *Definition of 'enervate.'* Collins Dictionary. collinsdictionary.com/dictionary/english/enervate

Collins Dictionary. (n.d.). *Definition of 'facultative.'* Collins Dictionary. https://www.collinsdictionary.com/us/dictionary/english/facultative

Collins Dictionary. (n.d.). *Definition of 'obligate.'* Collins Dictionary. collinsdictionary.com/dictionary/english/obligate

Collins Dictionary. (n.d.). *Definition of 'toxicosis.'* Collins Dictionary. collinsdictionary.com/dictionary/ english/toxicosis

REFERENCES

Covetrus: North America. (2016, September 6). *Canine Carnassial Teeth: Abscesses with Few Symptoms.* Covetrus: North America. northamerica.covetrus.com/resource-center/blogs/dentistry/dentistry/2016/09/06/canine-carnassial-teeth-abscesses-with-few-symptoms

The Darling Experiment Limited t/a Honey's Real Dog Food. (n.d). RAW PROOF: *The results of a 24-month research investigation into a species-appropriate diet for dog.* Self-Published. honeysrealdogfood.com/wordpress/wp-content/ uploads/2018/11/1026_Honeys_Raw-Proof-Report_A4 Spreads_ email.pdf

Dobbins, B. (January 3, 2017). *The Many Causes of Kennel Cough How do dogs get kennel cough?* Whole Dog Journal. https://www.whole-dog-journal.com/health/kennel-cough/the-many-causes-of-kennel-cough/

Dodds, J. (2017, December 9). *Dr. Jean Dodds – Dog Vaccine Protocol.* Animal Health Foundation. animalhealthfoundation.net/blog/2017/12/dr-jean-dodds-dog-vaccine-protocol/

Dogs First. (n.d.). *For Nice Teeth You Need To Cut Out The Dry Food And Feed Your Dog Raw Meaty Bones …* Dogs First. dogsfirst.ie/raw-faq/how-to-feed-a-dog-bones/

Dog Food Smart. (2020, July 17). *Chihuahua Growth Chart (Weight Chart) – When Do Chihuahuas Stop Growing?* Dog Food Smart. dogfoodsmart.com/chihuahua-growth-chart/

Dog Nutrition Naturally. (n.d.). *What Is the Difference Between Offal, Viscera and Organ Meats?* Dog Nutrition Naturally. dog-nutrition-naturally.com/offal.html

Domínguez-Oliva, A., Mota-Rojas, D., Semendric, I., Whittaker, A.L. (2023, January 12). *The Impact of Vegan Diets on Indicators of Health in Dogs and Cats: A Systematic Review.* Veterinary Sciences. https://doi.org/10.3390/vetsci10010052

Dreher, M. L. (2018, November 28). *Whole Fruits and Fruit Fiber Emerging Health Effects.* US National Library of Medicine National Institutes of Health. ncbi.nlm.nih.gov/pmc/articles/ PMC6315720/

Educalingo. (n.d.). *Definition of obligate.* Educalingo. https:// educalingo.com/en/dic-en/obligate

Encyclopedia Britannica. (n.d.). *Offal.* Encyclopedia Britannica. britannica.com/topic/offal

Eske, J. April 3, 2019. *How does oxidative stress affect the body?* Medical News Today. https://www.medicalnewstoday.com/articles/324863

Falconer, W. (2020, May 1). *Titer Testing Your Dog: Are You Wasting Your Money?* Dogs Naturally. dogsnaturallymagazine.com/titer-testing-dog/

Fetch by WedMD. (n.d.). *Rawhide: Good or Bad for Your Dog?* pets.webmd.com/dogs/rawhide-good-or-bad-for-your-dog#1

REFERENCES

Fontana L., Partridge L., Longo V.D. (2010, April 16). *Extending healthy life span--from yeast to humans.* Institutes of Health: National Library of Medicine National Center for Biotechnology Information. https://pubmed.ncbi.nlm.nih.gov/20395504

Ford, R., Larson, L., McClure, K., Schultz, R., Welborn, L. (October, 2017) 2017 AAHA *Canine Vaccination Guidelines. American Animal Hospital Association,* https://www.aaha.org/globalassets/02-guidelines/canine-vaccination/vaccination_recommendation_for_general_practice_table.pdf

Foundation Education. (2018, January 18). *What's the difference between free range and organic?* https://www.foundationeducation.edu.au/articles/free-range-vs-organic-whats-the-difference

Freeman, L. M. (2017, March 6). *Dietary Supplements for Pets: Harmful or Helpful?* Cummings Veterinary Medical Center at Tufts University. vetnutrition.tufts.edu/2017/03/dietary-supplements-for-pets-harmful-or-helpful/

The Free Dictionary by Farlex. (n.d.). *induration.* medical-dictionary.thefreedictionary.com/Induration

Harmful or Helpful? Cummings Veterinary Medical Center at Tufts University. vetnutrition.tufts.edu/2017/03/dietary-supplements-for-pets-harmful-or-helpful/

Gagne, M. (2020, October 29). *3 Reasons Your Dog Eats Grass and When To Be Worried.* Dogs Naturally. dogsnaturallymagazine.com/why-dogs-eat-grass/

Gander, K. (2020, January 16). *Wolf Pups Play Fetch Just Like Pet Dogs, Scientists Find.* Newsweek. newsweek.com/wolf-pups-play-fetch-just-like-pet-dogs-scientists-find-1482521

Gates, M. (2019, June 1). *Answers: What Exactly is an 'Obligate Carnivore?'* Feline Nutrition. feline-nutrition.org/answers/answers-what-exactly-is-an-obligate-carnivore

Get Smarter. (2020, February 14). *What are macronutrients and micronutrients.* getsmarter.com/blog/market-trends/what-are-macronutrients-and-micronutrients/

Gláucia B. P. N., Brunetto, M. A., Sousa, M. G., Carciofi, A. C., Camacho, A. A. (2010, April 5). *Effects of weight loss on the cardiac parameters of obese dogs.* SciELO. https://www.scielo.br/j/pvb/a/j7CJYNL8yZXz7j6L8q58z9v/?lang=en&format=html#

Goldhamer, A. (2010, 18 June). *How Your Body Heals Itself.* T. Colin Campbell Center For Nutrition Studies. nutritionstudies.org/body-heals/

Greenberg, S. M., Frazer, A. C., & Roberts, B. (1953, August 1). *Some Factors Affecting the Growth and Development of Rats Fed Rancid Fat.* Oxford Academic. academic.oup.com/jn/article-abstract/50/4/421/4726390?redirectedFrom=fulltext

Gunnars, K. (2018, June 11). *Why Care About Omega-6 and Omega-3 Fatty Acids?* Healthline. healthline.com/nutrition/optimize-omega-6-omega-3-ratio#TOC_TITLE_HDR_2

REFERENCES

HEALable. (2020). *Jicama Ingredient Guide.* healabel.com/j-ingredients/jicama

Health Science Journal. (n.d.). *About Health Science Journal.* Health Science Journal. hsj.gr/

Healthline. (n.d.). *Peanuts 101: Nutrition Facts and Health Benefits.* healthline.com/nutrition/foods/peanuts

Henriques, J. (2020, May 1). *5 Unexpected Dangers In Vaccines.* Dogs Naturally. dogsnaturallymagazine.com/5-unexpected-dangers-in-vaccines/

Hiperbaric High Pressure Processing. (n.d.). *What is High Pressure?* hiperbaric.com/en/high-pressure#:~:text=High%20Pressure%20Processing%20(HPP)%20is,87%2C000psi)%20transmitted%20by%20water

Hofve, J. (2020, November 19). *Raw Food Feeding Guide For Dogs And Cats.* Only Natural Pet. onlynaturalpet.com/blogs/holistic-healthcare-library/raw-food-feeding-guide-for-dogs-and-cats

Holistic Hound. (2016, October 3). *Raw Goat Milk Is Great For Your Dog.* holistichound.com/raw-goat-milk-is-great-for-your-dog/#:~:text=Raw%20goat%20milk%20is%20easy,provides%20even%20greater%20nutritional%20value

Holland, K. (2020, July 29). *Obesity Facts.* Healthline. healthline.com/health/obesity-facts

The Humane Society of the United States. (2010, May 20). *Pica: Why Pets Sometimes Eat Strange Objects.* Web Archive: Humane Society. web.archive.org/web/20160314025809/ https://www.wikihow.com/Treat-Pica-in-Older-Dogs

Iftikhar, N. (2019, January 14). *What Is Phage Therapy?* Healthline. https://www.healthline.com/health/phage-therapy

International Wolf Center. (n.d.). *Hunting And Feeding Behavior.* wolf.org/wolf-info/basic-wolf-info/biology-and-behavior/hunting-feeding-behavior/

International Wolf Center. (n.d.). *Wolf Pup Physical & Social Development.* wolf.org/wolf-info/basic-wolf-info/biology-and-behavior/pup-development/

Jordan, P. (2020, October 5). *Dangerous Over-Vaccination Is On The Rise.* Dogs Naturally. dogsnaturallymagazine.com/dangerous-over-vaccination-on-the-rise/

K9Natural. (n.d.). *A Load of Tripe.* k9natural.com/blogs/news/a-load-of-tripe

Kashef, Z. (2017, November 9). *A Very Low-Calorie Diet Reverses Type 2 Diabetes in People With Obesity.* Yale News. https://news.yale.edu/2017/11/09/study-reveals-how-very-low-calorie-diet-can-reverse-type-2-diabetes\

Kasprak, A. (2016, October 28). *Are Dogs Really 99.9% Wolf?* Snopes. snopes.com/fact-check/dogs-99-percent-wolf/

Kelly, J. (n.d.). *HOW MUCH DO WOLVES EAT ON AVERAGE?* Pets On Mom.com. animals.mom.com/much-wolves-eat-average-3840.html

Kim, B. (2019, September 9). *Rotational Feeding: A New Way of Feeding for Your Dog.* Zignature. zignature.com/rotational-feeding-a-new-way-of-feeding-for-your-dog/

Kraker, D. (2020, February 12). *New research from northern Minn. shows wolves feed berries to their young.* MPR News. mprnews.org/story/2020/02/12/new-research-from-northern-minn-shows-wolves-feed-berries-to-their-young

Krestel-Rickert, D. (September 17, 2018). *Time To Innovate — Specialty Pet Foods And Treats Offer Brands The Opportunity To Differentiate. Food Business News*

Kubala, J. (2020, August 12). *10 of the Best Foods to Help You Heal.* Healthline. healthline.com/nutrition/foods-that-help-you-heal

Learn The Risk Organization. (n.d.). *Pet Vaccines.* LearnTheRisk.org/pet-vaccines

Lease, E. J., Lease, J. G., Weber, J., & Steenbock, H. (1938, December 1). *Destruction of Vitamin A by Rancid Fats.* Oxford Academic. academic.oup.com/jn/article-abstract/16/6/571/4727049?redirectedFrom=fulltext

Legrand-Defretin, V. (1994). *Differences between cats and dogs: a nutritional view*. Cambridge University Press. https://www.cambridge.org/core/services/aop-cambridge-core/content/view/A01A77BABD1B6DDD500145D7A02D67A5/S0029665194000066a.pdf/differences-between-cats-and-dogs-a-nutritional-view.pdf

LeJeune, R. (n.d.). *LIVER & OTHER SECRETING ORGANS*. Perfectly Rawsome. perfectlyrawsome.com/raw-feeding-knowledgebase/liver-other-secreting-organs/#:~:text=Secreting%20%20organs%20are%20the%20most,organs%20in%20a%20raw%20diet

Lexico. (n.d.). *Meaning of obligate in English*. Lexico Powered By Oxford. lexico.com/definition/obligate

Link, R. (2018, January 6). *Amaranth: An Ancient Grain With Impressive Health Benefits*. Healthline. healthline.com/nutrition/amaranth-health-benefits

London, K. B. (2016, September). *Tips to Stop Your Dog from Eating Too Fast*. The Bark, Inc. thebark.com/content/tips-stop-your-dog-eating-too-fast

Longo V. D. & Fontana L. (2010, January 31). *Calorie restriction and cancer prevention: metabolic and molecular mechanisms*. Institutes of Health: National Library of Medicine National Center for Biotechnology Information. https://www.ncbi.nlm.nih.gov/pmc/articles/PMC2829867

REFERENCES

Marshall, A. (n.d.). *Raw Feeding Troubleshooting: My Dog's Not Interested In Raw Meat*. Primal Pooch. https://primalpooch.com/raw-feeding-troubleshooting-my-dogs-not-interested-in-raw-meat

Mattson, M.P. (2003, September 3). *Gene-diet interactions in brain aging and neurodegenerative disorders*. Institutes of Health: National Library of Medicine National Center for Biotechnology Information. https://pubmed.ncbi.nlm.nih.gov/12965973

Mech, L. D. (2007). *Wolves: Behavior, Ecology, and Conservation* (L. Boitani, Ed.; New edition ed., Vol. 2). University of Chicago Press

Merriam-Webster. (n.d.). *Definition*. merriam-webster.com/dictionary/ruminants

Meyers, H. (2022, August 2). *Why Does My Dog Eat Grass?* American Kennel Club. akc.org/expert-advice/health/why-does-my-dog-eat-grass/

Mlacnik, E., Bockstahler, B.A., Müller, M., Tetrick, M.A., Nap, R.C., & Zentek, J. (2006, December 1). *Effects of caloric restriction and a moderate or intense physiotherapy program for treatment of lameness in overweight dogs with osteoarthritis*. Journal of the American Veterinary Medical Association. https://doi.org/10.2460/javma.229.11.1756

Monogastrics VS Ruminants (PDF). (n.d.). http://brincksm.weebly.com/. http://brincksm.weebly.com/uploads/3/6/3/4/3634133/communication_artifact.pdf

Myers, W. S. (2020, May 8). *When clients question your pharmacy prices*. Veterinary Practice News. veterinarypracticenews.com/internet-pharmacies-may-2020/

Myers, P., R. Espinosa, C. S., Parr, T., Jones, G. S. Hammond, and Dewey, T. A. (2023). The Animal Diversity Web (online). https://animaldiversity.org/accounts/Canis_lupus_familiaris/classification

National Center for Biotechnology Information, U.S. National Library of Medicine. (2014, October 22). *Nasal immunity is an ancient arm of the mucosal immune system of vertebrates*

National Center for Biotechnology Information, U.S. National Library of Medicine. ncbi.nlm.nih.gov/pmc/articles/PMC4321879/

National Peanut Board. (n.d.). *Can Peanut Butter Harm Your Dog? An Expert Weighs in for National Dog Day*. nationalpeanutboard.org/news/can-peanut-butter-kill-your-dog-an-expert-weighs-in-for-national-dog-day.htm

National Research Council. (2006). *Nutrient Requirements of Dogs and Cats (Nutrient Requirements of Animals)* Illustrated edition (July 1, 2006). National Academies Press

The National Wildlife Federation. (n.d.). Gray Wolf. https://www.nwf.org/Educational-Resources/Wildlife-Guide/Mammals/Gray-Wolf

REFERENCES

Only Natural Pet. (2020, July 28). *Raw Food Feeding Guide For Dogs And Cats.* Only Natural Pet. onlynaturalpet.com/blogs/holistic-healthcare-library/raw-food-feeding-guide-for-dogs-and-cats

O'Rourke, A. (2020, October 19). *Overweight Covid Risk Get your BMI to find out!* Covid Science Blog. covidscienceblog.com/overweight-covid-risk-get-your-bmi-to-find-out/

Oxford University Press. (n.d.). *Antigen.* Oxford Learner's Dictionary. oxfordlearnersdictionaries.com/us/definition/english/antigen

Paretts, S. (2019, August 16). *When Does My Puppy Finish Growing?* American Kennel Club. akc.org/expert-advice/health/when-does-my-puppy-finish-growing/

Patton, R. (April 30, 2013). *What to Feed Your Dog.* Dr. Richard Patton Animal Nutrition. https://pattonanimalnutrition.com/what-to-feed-your-dog/

Pavcek, P. L., & Shull, G. M. (1953, September 5). Inactivation Of Biotin By Rancid Fats. *Journal: (From the Department of Biochemistry, College of Agriculture, University of Wisconsin, Madison),* NA, 6. jbc.org/content/146/2/351.full.pdf

Peralta, J. (2020, October 6). *5 Reasons Dogs Eat Dirt.* Dogs Naturally. dogsnaturallymagazine.com/5-reasons-dogs-eat-dirt/

Perfectly Rawsome Website. (n.d.). *Calculate An Estimated Raw Feeding Monthly Budget.* Retrieved from https://perfectlyrawsome.com/raw-feeding-knowledgebase/calculate-estimated-raw-feeding-monthly-budget/

Perkins S. N., Hursting, S. D., Phang, J.M., & Haines D.C. (1998, August). *Calorie restriction reduces ulcerative dermatitis and infection-related mortality in p53-deficient and wild-type mice.* Institutes of Health: National Library of Medicine National Center for Biotechnology Information. https://pubmed.ncbi.nlm.nih.gov/9699732

Perry, R.J., Peng, L., Cline, G.W., Wang, Y., Rabin-Court, A., Song, J.D., Zhang, D., Zhang, X.-M., Nozaki, Y., Dufour, S., Petersen, K.F., and Shulman, G.I. (2017, November 9). *Mechanisms by which a Very-Low-Calorie Diet Reverses Hyperglycemia in a Rat Model of Type 2 Diabetes.* Cell Metabolism. https://www.cell.com/cell-metabolism/fulltext/S1550-4131(17)30616-2

Pet Health Network. (n.d.). *Dog Diseases & Conditions A-Z.* Pet Health Network. pethealthnetwork.com/dog-health/dog-diseases-conditions-a-z

Pets WebMD. (n.d.). *Fevers in Cats.* pets.webmd.com/cats/fevers-in-cats#1

Raw and Fresh. (2020, March 5*). Raw Feeding Guide for Dogs.* rawandfresh.com.au/blogs/blog/how-much-raw-food-should-i-feed-my-dog

REFERENCES

Raw Fed Dogs. (n.d.). *A Starter Guide.* Raw Fed Dogs. http://rawfeddogs.org/rawguide

The Raw Feeding Community. (2019, June 17). *How Much Does It Cost To Feed Raw?* The Raw Feeding Community. therawfeedingcommunity.com/2018/03/11/how-much-does-it-cost-to-feed-raw/

ReAct Group. (n.d.). *UNDERSTAND – BACTERIA: Essential for life.* reactgroup.org/toolbox/understand/bacteria/bacteria-are-essential-for-human-life/

Reardon, Z. (n.d.). *At What Age Do German Shepherds Stop Growing?* Embora Pets. emborapets.com/at-what-age-do-german-shepherds-stop-growing/

Richmond, M. (2014, 2020). *Titer Testing: An alternative to annual vaccines for dogs.* The Bark. thebark.com/content/titer-testing

Ripley, K. (2018, July 26). *Can Dogs Eat Potatoes?* American Kennel Club. akc.org/expert-advice/nutrition/can-dogs-eat-potatoes/

Robertson, R. (2020, October 22). *Omega-3-6-9 Fatty Acids: A Complete Overview.* Healthline. healthline.com/nutrition/omega-3-6-9-overview#food-sources

Romero, M. (2012, October 25). *6 Fruits and Vegetables With Healing Powers.* Washingtonian. washingtonian.com/2012/10/25/6-fruits-and-vegetables-with-healing-powers/

Rotkovitz, M. (2020, September 17). *What Is a Pseudocereal or Non-Cereal Grain?* The Spruce Eats. thespruceeats.com/what-is-a-pseudocereal-1664721

Saba, C.F. (January 12, 2017). V*accine-associated feline sarcoma: current perspectives.* US National Library of Medicine National Institutes of Health. https://www.ncbi.nlm.nih.gov/pmc/articles/PMC6042530/

Savory Prime Pet. (n.d.). *Six Essential Nutrients Dogs Need.* Savory Prime Pet Treats. savoryprimepet.com/lets-talk-dog-nutrition-6-essential-nutrients-dogs-need/

Scanlan, N. (2011, July 11). *The Health Benefits Of Therapeutic Fasting.* Veterinary Practice News. veterinarypracticenews.com/the-health-benefits-of-therapeutic-fasting/

Schultz, R. (2003, March 14). Schultz: *Dog vaccines may not be necessary.* University Of Wisconsin–Madison News. news.wisc.edu/schultz-dog-vaccines-may-not-be-necessary/

Schultz, Ronald. (February 12, 2016). *Canine Antibody Testing: Frequently Asked Questions. School of Veterinary Medicine, University of Wisconsin-Madison.* https://www.vetmed.wisc.edu/lab/wp-content/uploads/sites/12/2016/02/Canine-Antibody-FAQ.pdf

Science Daily. (n.d.). *Reference Terms: Health science.* sciencedaily.com/terms/health_science.htm

Scitable By Nature Education. (2014). *Definition: Bacteriophage.* nature.com/scitable/definition/bacteriophage-phage-293/#:~:text=A%20bacteriophage%20is%20a%20type,surrounded%20by%20a%20 protein%20structure

Scott, D. (2017, September 26). *How Long Does Kibble Last? Dogs Naturally.* https://www.dogsnaturallymagazine.com/throw-dogs-kibble-away

Scott, D. (2019, May 19). *The Stink On Tripe: Does Your Dog Need It?* Dogs Naturally. dogsnaturallymagazine.com/the-stink-on-tripe

Scott, D. (2022, August 26). *The #1 Mistake Raw Feeders Make With Organ Meats. Dogs Naturally.* https://www.dogsnaturallymagazine.com/mistake-raw-feeders-make-with-organ-meats

Scott, D. (2020, March 16). *Five Dangerous Dog Vaccine Ingredients.* Dogs Naturally Magazine. dogsnaturallymagazine.com/five-vaccine-ingredients-that-can-harm-your-dog/

Scott, D. (2020, November 2). *Raw Fish And Parasites. Dogs Naturally.* dogsnaturallymagazine.com/raw-fish-and-parasites/

Scully, S. (2017, March 27). *Why wolves mate for life and 22 other interesting things to know about these animals.* Upworthy. upworthy.com/why-wolves-mate-for-life-and-22-other-interesting-things-to-know-about-these-animals

Shagoury, K. (2017, March 15). *Inflammation could be the cause of all disease, researcher says.* Integrative Practitioner. integrativepractitioner.com/practice-management/news/inflammation-could-be-the-cause-of-all-disease

Stahler, D. R., Smith, D. W., & Guernsey, D. S. (2006, July). *Foraging and feeding ecology of the gray wolf (Canis lupus): lessons from Yellowstone National Park, Wyoming, USA.* National Center for Biotechnology Information, U.S. National Library of Medicine. https://pubmed.ncbi.nlm.nih.gov/16772460/

Stebbins, N. (2019, November 8). *Rawhide Bones: The Good, The Bad and The Downright Dangerous.* Canine Journal. caninejournal.com/rawhide-bones/#:~:text=In%20countries%20outside%20of%20the,an%20extra%20dose%20of%20chemicals

Sterbenz, C. (2014, March 24). *13 Surprising Things That Are Partly Made From Animal Products.* Business Insider. businessinsider.com/15-surprising-things-that-contain-animal-products-2014-3?r=MX&IR=T

Steve's Real Food. (2015). *The Cost to Feed Raw Pet Food.* stevesrealfood.com/2015/06/03/the-cost-to-feed-raw-pet-food/

Suzuki, S. (1987, October). *Experimental studies on the presumption of the time after food intake from stomach contents.* National Institutes of Health: National Library of Medicine National Center for Biotechnology Information. pubmed.ncbi.nlm.nih.gov/3428803/

REFERENCES

Szalay, J. (2015, December 18). *What Is Dietary Fat?* Live Science. livescience.com/53145-dietary-fat.html

Szalay, J. (2018, April 19). *Quinoa: Health Benefits & Nutrition Facts.* Live Science. livescience.com/50400-quinoa-nutrition-facts.html#:~:text=Often%20used%20as%20a%20substitute,in%20a%20story%20for%20NPR

Tollden Farms. (n.d.). *Making the Switch to a Raw Food Diet.* tolldenfarms.ca/learning-centre/making-the-switch-to-a-raw-food-diet#feeding-cats

True Carnivores staff. (n.d.). *Bone Feeding Guide.* True Carnivores. truecarnivores.com/learning-centre/bone-feeding-guide/

U.S. Department of Agriculture. (n.d.). Agricultural Research Service. FoodData Central Search Results. https://fdc.nal.usda.gov/fdc-app.html#/?query=food%20calculator

U.S. Food and Drug Administration. (2017, November 29). *What You Need to Know about Dietary Supplements.* https://www.fda.gov/consumers/consumer-updates/fda-101-dietary-supplements

US National Library of Medicine National Institutes of Health. (2000, September). *Autoimmune diseases: a leading cause of death among young and middle-aged women in the United States.* US National Library of Medicine National Institutes of Health. ncbi.nlm.nih.gov/pmc/articles/PMC1447637/

Virbac UK. (n.d.). *Your Cat's Teeth Explained.* uk.virbac.com/home/advice/pagecontent/health-topics/your-cats-teeth-explained.html

WebMD. (n.d.). *Slideshow: Foods Your Dog Should Never Eat* pets.webmd.com/dogs/risky-foods

Wernimont, S. M., Radosevich, J., Jackson, M. I., Ephraim, E., Badri, D. V., MacLeay, J. M., Jewell, D. E., & Suchodolski, J. S. (2020, June 25). *The Effects of Nutrition on the Gastrointestinal Microbiome of Cats and Dogs: Impact on Health and Disease.* US National Library of Medicine National Institutes of Health Search. ncbi.nlm.nih.gov/pmc/articles/PMC7329990/

Western Wildlife Outreach. (n.d.). *Wolf Ecology and Behavior: Wolf Diet.* http://westernwildlife.org/gray-wolf-outreach-project/biology-behavior-4/

Wikipedia. (n.d.). Definition of 'monogastric.' Wikipedia. https://en.wikipedia.org/wiki/Monogastric

Wikipedia. (n.d.). Definition of 'orthopathy.' Wikipedia. https://en.wikipedia.org/wiki/Orthopathy

Wikipedia. (n.d.). Definition of 'rendering.' Wikipedia. https://en.wikipedia.org/wiki/Rendering_(animal_products)

Wikipedia. (n.d.). Definition of 'millets.' Wikipedia. https://en.wikipedia.org/wiki/Millet

REFERENCES

Wolf Park. (n.d.). *Wolves.* wolfpark.org/animals/wolves/?fbclid=IwAR25HIZnBxL8y8g-97zqpublY7SAvk6EnZ8ANUgrJvb8w0z9R3OlGeg2TFc

World Population Review. (2020). *Most Obese Countries 2020.* worldpopulationreview.com/country-rankings/most-obese-countries

Zvi, A. (n.d.). *Organic Vs. Free-Range Chicken.* SFGate. homeguides.sfgate.com/organic-vs-freerange-chicken-79168.html

AFFILIATE DISCLAIMER

I AM GRATEFUL TO BE OF SERVICE and bring you certain content free of charge. To do this, please note that when you click on product links provided in this book and purchase items, in some cases, I will receive a referral commission. You will not pay more when buying a product through my link.

I only recommend products and systems I use and love myself, or my peers have used and recommended, so I know you'll be in good hands, and if helps not to have to reinvent the wheel each time you need a recommendation. Your support in purchasing through these links, enables me to keep my web hosting and customization costs within a manageable range. I thank you profusely for your support.

The Catalyst Group, Inc., is a participant in the Amazon Services, LLC Associates Program, an affiliate advertising program designed to provide a means for sites to earn advertising fees by advertising and linking to amazon.com, as well as many other affiliate programs.

As directed by the Federal Trade Commission, (see 16 CFR Part 255) – Guides Concerning the Use of Endorsements and Testimonials in Advertising, the purpose of this policy is to establish any compensatory affiliation between the site owner and others listed above.

The compensation received may or may not influence the advertising content, topics, or posts made on this site. That content, advertising

Space, or post may not always be identified as paid or sponsored content. Not all content is written or presented for the sole purpose of receiving affiliate income. Clicking on links or purchasing products contained on this website may generate income for this website's owner(s).

ABOUT THE AUTHOR

DR. STEPHANIE KROL is past Dean of Schools in higher education for for-profit Allied Health Schools, and currently a co-owner of a Real Estate School, a Certified Publishing Services Provider and Hybrid Publisher. Prior to earning her Doctorate in Education, she was on the path to become an Equine Veterinarian. From her teenage years and on, she rode horses professionally. She earned many Jumper, Rally, and Dressage awards. She even finished one score short of a bronze medal in Dressage. The unattainable final point was due to her horse's degenerative disease not being fully cured enough after surgery to earn the big marks she needed, but gratefully enough to keep him out of pain after surgery for his lifetime.

At 16 years old, Stephanie moved on to becoming a trained Veterinary Technician and Laboratory Technician. She held those roles through the first two years of college while then earning her first college degree in Psychology.

While participating in equestrian events for a couple of decades, she earned her C3 level as a Pony Clubber (which is a prep program for kids who want to have careers in Equine fields).

Much later on, once she moved on from her career in Higher Education, she moved on to Certified Health and Wellness Coaching and became a Functional Medicine Practitioner while also co-owning a real estate school.

Dr. Krol also holds a Certification in Animal Behavior for Dogs, Cats and Rabbits. She holds a Professional Status and is a Member of the International Association of Canine Professionals and is certified with the Commission for the Association of Drugless Practitioners. She also is a Certified Raw Dog Food Nutrition Specialist from DNM University.

For the latest updates or to contact her for consultations, reach out to Dr. Stephanie Krol at:

Email: questions@catalystgroupsolutions.com
Dog Page: facebook.com/dogwellnesscoaching
Author Page: facebook.com/Stephanie-Krol-100230538923667
Website: wellnessandhealthnow.com/about-the-book
Pet products I use or peers use:
wellnessandhealthnow.com/pet-products/
Consultation Services can be paid for and found here toward the bottom of this page:
wellnessandhealthnow.com/work-with-me/

www.ingramcontent.com/pod-product-compliance
Lightning Source LLC
Chambersburg PA
CBHW071225080526

44587CB00013BA/1498